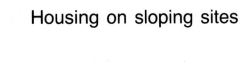

Housing on sloping sites

General Editor: Colin Bassett, BSc, FCIOB, FFB

Related titles
Tree Roots and Buildings, *D Cutler and I B K Richardson*
House Construction, *National Building Agency*
Site Costs in Housing Development, *B J Simpson*
Structural Recommendations for Timber Frame Housing, *Timber Research and Development Association (TRADA)*
Timber Frame Housing Manual, *Timber Research and Development Association (TRADA)*

Housing on sloping sites:
a design guide
B J Simpson and M T Purdy

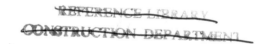

Construction Press
London and New York

Construction Press
an imprint of:
Longman Group Limited
Longman House, Burnt Mill, Harlow
Essex CM20 2JE, England
Associated companies throughout the world

*Published in the United States of America
by Longman Inc., New York*

First published 1984

British Library Cataloguing in Publication Data

Simpson, Barry J.
 Housing on sloping sites.
 1. Architecture, Domestic — Great Britain
 2. Hillside architecture — Great Britain
 I. Title   II. Purdy, M. T.
 728.3   NA7328

ISBN 0-86095-041-7

Library of Congress Cataloging in Publication Data

Simpson, Barry J., 1948–
 Housing on sloping sites.

 Bibliography: p.
 Includes index.
 1. Dwellings.   2. Hillside architecture.   I. Purdy,
M. T. (Martin Terence), 1939–   II. Title.
NA7524.S55   1984   728   83–27212
ISBN 0-86095-041-7

Set in Linotron 202 10/12 Plantin

Printed in Great Britain at The Pitman Press, Bath

Contents

Preface

During the last decade many design guides for housing have been written. Most cover only a limited range of house design – principally extensions and conversions – and many are hardly known outside the local authority where they were produced. The best-known guide, prepared by Melvin Dunbar and others for Essex County Council in 1973, is, of course, for a county known for its flatness and says very little about slopes. In fact, despite so much having been written about house design, slopes are seldom featured. It is quite inexplicable why so much design guidance is two dimensional, while so many sites are significantly three dimensional. The few works addressed to slopes (for example, *Hill Housing* (Abbott and Pollit 1980) and *Häuser am Hang* (Wolff 1981)) are mostly about specially designed 'one-off' houses, usually on slopes steeper than about 9° (1 in 6). Mass housing on more gentle slopes has had little attention. It is our intention to remedy that in this book.

Design practice in the UK for housing on slopes has been very variable in recent years. A majority of those cases we have met, in both public and private sectors, have been 'designed' (built), paying as little attention to slope as possible. Frequently, slopes of up to perhaps 5° to 7° (1 in 11 to 1 in 8) have been regarded as a nuisance which would add to the cost of construction, resulting in awkward changes of level in site layouts. The ground has simply been gouged out to form little flat platforms for the same little boxes as on any other site. On steeper slopes, the folly of this has been made clear to most, but not all, developers and they have either avoided such sites, as in the case of the large private sector developers, or used other designs.

Not all developers have ignored the opportunities of sloping sites. Several of the larger local authorities and a few smaller ones too have developed house designs and site layouts which are aesthetically more in harmony with their surroundings, take advantage of fine views, sunlight, privacy and other opportunities and frequently save money as well. A few private developers, particularly the smaller ones with no notions of mass production, have also developed some interesting ideas, frequently on awkward sites left to them as a result of their weaker bargaining position.

The layout and design of an estate on a slope seems to depend more on who develops it than on the nature of the site itself. We do not pretend that there is a 'best design' for any site. Nevertheless, much of what we have seen could have been better achieved by a different developer. Of course, what is best for one developer is not necessarily the case for another. Much depends on the way the firm is organized. However, the acceptability of what we have seen could certainly be questioned by those who have to live with the results. This variability in practice should cause concern to planners and others who control design. Some may be justifiable according to variations in organizational practice between developers – public and private, large and small – especially in a field so dependent upon taste and opinion. Nevertheless, the radically different responses are not dependent either on site characteristics or on demonstrated consumer preference, but on the developer. This, we feel, is too much to accept without question. There are problems both of lack of dissemination of practice and experience between developers, public and private, and lack of choice available to consumers. To what extent do house buyers really want the houses that are presented to them? Would other designs sell at least as well if they were offered?

This book is intended for all those professional officers who are involved in site planning and house design in the process of land development. Chapter 3 on site planning may well appeal primarily to town planners. Architects may see their main interest reflected in Chapter 4. Surveyors may find their interests divided between the two with some of their particular interests reflected in Chapter 6. Landscape architects may be primarily concerned with aspects related to earthworks (Ch. 5) but should also find material of interest in Chapter 4 on house design and perhaps even more so in Chapter 3 on site planning. The first two chapters serve as an introduction to the opportunities of sloping sites for housing and the physical constraints which must be considered by any profession.

To all these professions we have addressed our guidance in the form of principles distilled from examples of recent good practice. We have avoided the temptation to design housing or layouts for hypothetical or real sites, or even to go into excessive detail about the examples we have chosen. Good design is not achieved by merely providing a template but will be a creation of our readers. We simply hope to offer some ideas to fuel this creative process with some results of the experiences of others.

During the preparation of this work we have relied on the generous way in which many officers in local authorities and the private sector have contributed their time and experiences. We are particularly grateful to Mr W Howland of Birmingham City Architect's Department; Mr Michael Deakin, Architect, of Looe, Cornwall; Mr Peter Phippen of Phippen, Randall and Parkes, Architects of East Molesey, Surrey; Mr Bernard Griffiths, Superintending Quantity Surveyor of the Housing Directorate at the Department of the Environment; Mr Graham Reddie, Mr David Bates and Mr Charles Holmes of Redditch Development Corporation; Mr Jack Owen and Mr Patrick Todd of Wimpey Construction UK Ltd; Mr K Hawtin of Barratt Developments (Sutton Coldfield) Ltd; Mr Keith Gray of Wates Homes Ltd; Mr John Hope of John Laing & Co. (Bristol); Mr Stephen Lowe and Mr David Clare of Bovis Homes Ltd; Mr Ralph Lebens; Mr R Parr of Burnley

Borough Engineer's Department; Mr Paul Weston of the Charter Design Group of Banbury; Mr Riley of Rileyform Ltd; Mr John Wythe of the John Stedman Design Group; Dr John Gibbons of the Scottish Development Department; Mr H Powell and Mr R Howse of Cwmbran Development Corporation; Mr Keith Mower of Hawkes and Braby, Quantity Surveyors; and Mr Nigel Evans of Cherwell District Council. Also, we are most grateful for research help from Mrs Anne Upton, Miss Heather Morrison and Miss Julia Butter and to Mr Colin Bassett and the staff of Longman for their constant help and advice. Finally, we must acknowledge the generous sponsorship of a research project by the Science and Engineering Research Council on the effects of land slope and soil composition on house construction costs, carried out by ourselves at Aston University, and Professor Denys Hinton for his support on this project.

Barry J. Simpson
Martin Purdy
July 1983

Acknowledgements

Figs. 3.8, 3.10, 4.59, 6.1 and 7.1 are reproduced by kind permission of *The Surveyor* (IPC Building and Contract Journals Ltd).

Chapter 1

Introduction – issues in housing on slopes

Current practices for housing on slopes

Professional officers and politicians and perhaps the house-buying public too are becoming more conscious of house design and the possibilities of good site planning. Design guides have proliferated from local authorities during the last decade. Even the criticism of mass housing design of late indicates the concern that is felt. Aesthetically, schemes are often described as monotonous, lacking in local identity and having no appreciation of immediate 'place'. Technically they have been attacked for using inappropriate means of construction, shoddy materials and poor detailing.

Large-scale housing layouts are often a crude aggregate of smaller parts, put together from standard design components conceived in isolation from their setting and future inhabitants. Such insensitivity of approach and shortcomings in design are exacerbated in schemes on sloping land where the prominence of the third dimension highlights such failings. Plans designed in the vacuum of the drawing office and on a flat piece of paper translate badly into the subtle demands of varying contours. In such circumstances the importance of silhouette, skyline, roofscape, building junctions and, most crucial, the handling of spaces between houses, is vital.

In the UK there is evidence that the proportion of housing situated on slopes is increasing, perhaps due to the shortage of flat land, or to an increasing concern to preserve good agricultural land (which is usually flat), maybe even because housing on slopes is becoming increasingly sought after. Department of the Environment statistics reveal that over the period from March 1976 to March 1980 the proportion of public sector housing schemes which were granted *ad hocs* for site conditions rose only slightly from 46 per cent to 48 per cent, whereas over the same period the total amount granted rose by 79 per cent.

A number of shortcomings are common in design on slopes:

1. *Visual factors.* Design of whatever standard is usually emphasized on hills. Skyline and silhouette are prominent and the placing of garages and the relationship of access to individual buildings is often awkward.

2. *Positive use of site.* The majority of solutions are standard flat-site boxes

1

Fig. 1.1 Excessive terracing across the slope creates changes of level between adjacent houses – Pool Farm Estate, Birmingham

Fig. 1.2 Fussy and expensive stepping of individual houses and crudely screened, vandal-prone garage court – Pool Farm Estate, Birmingham

squeezed on to manipulated terraces with steep changes of level between inconsistent steps and ramps.

3. *Massing*. Slopes draw attention to and aggravate awkward junctions within and between buildings: an aesthetic and economic problem.

4. *Internal layout.*The opportunity to achieve fine views, interesting rooms and natural privacy are sometimes forgone either due to poor design work or the desire to squeeze more housing on to the site. The advantages offered by

Fig. 1.3 Doing their best to ignore the slope and any opportunities it might offer, these houses at Dudley, West Midlands, march straight up the hillside

Fig. 1.4 A classic example of 'step and stagger' terrace.

Fig. 1.5 Steep hillsides provide an opportunity to emphasize the individuality of large houses and to make them even more commanding and dramatic. In this case, the long sweeps of the roofline of this house at Burton-upon-Trent seem almost to provide a summit for the hillside

sloping sites to achieve interesting spaces within the dwelling are usually ignored: views from within the dwelling are usually ignored: views from within the dwelling are often worse than on the level, perhaps looking out on to a high retaining wall, steep embankment or the roofs of other houses downslope.

5. *Privacy.* Overlooking from upslope has led to loss of privacy or high, ugly and expensive walls to prevent this. With thoughtful design, this loss can even be reversed on hill slopes.

6. *Landscaping.* Steep gardens may be of limited use and awkward to maintain. Where earthworks have been part of the solution to building, some sections will be even steeper than in the natural state. Often, it is a case of flattening the parts of the site covered by building, resulting in even steeper gardens. Sometimes these can be so steep that there is even a considerable loss of daylight and frequently the outlooks from the houses are marred by steep embankments only a few feet away from main windows.

7. *External works.* Retaining walls are a problem. They are usually detrimental visually and often very expensive to construct. In some situations they are also an open invitation to graffiti and cause noise reverberation, as when leading on to a court of garages.

8. *Vehicular access.* Steep driveways are more difficult to use and can even limit the size of car.

Fig. 1.6 High (and expensive) retaining wall leading on to a court of garages in private sector housing at Sutton Coldfield, West Midlands. This must cause some noise reverberation and restrict the outlook from the houses downslope. Palisade type fences enclose the back gardens of houses upslope in this exposed, windy position

Fig. 1.7 Private sector housing at Sutton Coldfield, West Midlands. Garage court and retaining wall. Downslope the individual garage minimizes the impact of the wall, helps reduce construction costs of the garage and also provides a use for part of the retaining wall where any damp penetration would be less serious than with living accommodation

9. *Costs*. Substructure costs are often excessive and opportunities of reducing them are missed.

10. *Energy conservation*. Lack of consideration for the effects of built form on energy losses – certain shapes of house shell such as wide frontage/shallow depth houses built along the contours have a large surface area for heat losses; so too do steps and staggers in terraces, introduced to negotiate slope. The possibilities of increasing thermal insulation by building partly into the slope has had very little attention in the UK.

Fig. 1.8 Flat site houses on manipulated terraces: Sutton Coldfield

Fig. 1.9 Skyline development, Bradford. The monotony of design, bad enough on the level, is emphasized on a slope.

11. *SLOAP* (*space left over after planning*) – useless spaces left over in site
planning sometimes due to unwillingness to adapt house design or areas
regarded as being too steep for building, as a result of earthworks.

Fig. 1.10 Cut-and-fill on what is already a steep slope makes left-over spaces, usually
gardens or verges, even steeper, and more awkward to use. Some rooms look out on to a
grass embankment (or the underside of a car) and must lose some privacy unless hidden by
bushes, making the daylighting problem even worse. Harborne, Birmingham

Fig. 1.11 Many planning authorities would not give permission for a detached garage in
front of the building line. Even on a flat site they would usually dominate the appearance
of the street. Flat site designs on a slope are even worse and not made any better by being
built at the same time as the house. Banbury, Oxfordshire

7

Fig. 1.12 The need to accommodate vehicles within the curtilage of each plot can result in private driveways with steep exhaust-scraping slopes. Cwmbran, Gwent

Fig. 1.13 A large open space with no obvious use adds to the bleakness of this scheme at Blackburn, Lancashire

Fig. 1.14 Multi-storey housing can be used in a positive way to overcome the problem of sloping sites, but in contrast with the bold layout of the eighteenth century city, these recent flats in Ballance Street, Bath, sited close to two of the most famous crescents, assault the slope in a crude manner.

An effort has been made to match the materials of the older houses, and car parking is tucked beneath the roof terraces, but the overall result is a ponderous and insensitive solution to this particular locality

Faulty house design and site planning such as these examples stem from a failure to adapt to gradient – schemes are adapted in two dimensions with little regard to height and then the site is flattened section by section by earthworks. Slope appears to be regarded as a nuisance to be overcome rather than as an opportunity to be exploited.

Fig. 1.15 Private sector housing at Burton-upon-Trent showing several disadvantages of designs which ignore slope:
— steep driveways
— steep gardens perhaps giving a claustrophobic effect and loss of privacy to ground floor living rooms
— loss of privacy to the patio at first floor level
— the high blank wall of next door's garage causing even more shadowing than it would have done on the level

Fig. 1.16 Indecision at Stourbridge, West Midlands. Two-storey houses with massive earth retention, or three-storey flats?

The effects of the type of developer

Research carried out by the authors for the Science and Engineering Research Council has shown that adaptation to the special opportunities and constraints of slopes is most common amongst the larger local authorities, who may have staff available for design, and the smaller private sector developers who cannot take advantage of mass-produced housing which mostly deters large private sector developers from adapting house form. The justification for the wide variation in practice is weak. It is certainly influenced by a number of factors other than site characteristics.

To some extent, particularly among the large private sector developers, this unwillingness to have regard to gradient, both in terms of house design and site layout, may be the result of lack of interest as well as lack of appreciation. House buyers, building societies and the housing market are generally conservative. Developers are not surprisingly sceptical of the financial returns which would result from design effort and the (supposed) disruption that might arise from their mass production procedures. It may seem far safer to limit innovation to 'Georgian' front doors, fitted kitchens and glass fibre columns tacked on to standard houses. To what extent house buyers are getting what they want and how they are conditioned by availability coupled with a 'safe' investment, is far from certain. However, it is apparent that very little market research has been done in the UK apart from the knowledge that, in purely economic terms, the present practice works.

Design, however, is not only the concern of the house buyer and the developer. External appearance is the province of the planning authority. There is no doubt that during the last decade many local authorities have become more appreciative of estate design and site planning, but more seems to have been achieved in public sector mass housing than in the private sector. The economic objectives and constraints within which they work are probably more uniform between local authorities than between private sector developers. Nevertheless, practice on slopes is at least as varied in the public as the private sector. It seems beyond reasonable doubt that there is a large measure of lack of awareness of house design and site layout possibilities on slopes and how these can be made to comply with central Government regulations for cost control. This relaxation in cost yardstick controls in the public sector (Department of the Environment 1981) could provide opportunities for innovation, though the housing cost yardstick has not stifled imagination in all authorities. As 'value' is now the determining factor it is to be hoped that this will be interpreted in the longer term to avoid temporary economic solutions.

Inefficiency in the design process

Standardization economies have been given as a reason for reluctance to adapt house design among several of the large private sector developers. When design is incorporated into slope, for most developers it is a 'one off' study. The possibilities of standardization for slopes therefore hardly seems to have started. One obstacle is the lack of information of the experience gained. Despite the vast literature on house design and planning, very little is devoted to slopes and even less is concerned with mass housing on such sites. Why so much of the literature is two dimensional while so many sites are significantly three dimensional is inexplicable.

Aims of this study

In designing housing and site planning on slopes, several factors need to be considered including the following:

1. *Aesthetic awareness of the third dimension*: massing and silhouette, prospect and aspect.

2. *Density and efficiency of layout*: left-over unused spaces.

3. *Initial costs of construction*, external works, landscaping and services.

4. *Costs-in-use*: maintenance of the house fabric, energy efficiency. Heating costs are considerably affected by the shape of the house shell. Sometimes, savings in capital costs are at the expense of little understood costs-in-use.

5. *Site maintenance*: unusual landscaping, upkeep of retaining walls, difficult grass cutting.

These factors can be considered by designers only within the context of a number of specialized technical, administrative and legal considerations. Geotechnics, including soil, water tables, loading capacities, and climatology (for example, radiation exposure, shadowing, local wind circulations and cold air drainage) can be extremely important. All of these constraints are also subject to the requirements for planning permission, which although similar include emphasis on the effects of appearance and use on neighbours and neighbourhood. Like planning permission, land acquisition costs are an essential consideration which will, to some extent, reflect the factors already mentioned. Usually they will reflect extra costs of site difficulties, though they have sometimes resulted in cheaper units at high density to recoup outlay on land purchase. The market potential of house design and perhaps to a lesser extent consumer preferences concerning site layouts are also important considerations for the house designer and developer.

A local authority has a duty to consider all of the factors already mentioned in this section, for even market price will have an effect on whether or not housing need is satisfied. But it usually has an inadequate basis on which to do so. It may regard the appearance of an estate as adequate but open to improvement. Few planning authorities have the knowledge available of what house forms *are* possible; even fewer have data on the full range of implications of either their own house designs of those of the private sector. This applies particularly to costs-in-use. They do not have an adequate basis either to make decisions on their own public housing or for development control decisions in the private sector.

The general aim of this work is therefore to provide guidance for house design and site planning on sloping land, concentrating on the shortcomings which have been identified in current practice. This guidance is intended for those professions involved in the housing development process in the public, private and housing association sectors.

Our approach is to compare good practice to date with a view to identifying and appreciating the range of design and planning possibilities. Criteria for choice within these possibilities will be presented as responses to house type requirements, soil conditions, angle and direction of slope.

There are several policy implications for both the control of house design and site planning by both local and central government and for innovation by designers and planners in all sectors. We hope therefore, that our book will also offer guidance in several policy areas:

(a) To promote greater appreciation of the difficulties and opportunities associated with sloping sites by developers in all sectors but particularly those which cannot employ adequate professional staff; for example, small housing associations. We do not seek to impose a design orthodoxy, but to promote appreciation of standards, criteria and guidelines for choice.

(b) To guide development control standards in local planning authorities.

(c) To assist judgements on what is reasonable subsidy for public housing by central government and other organizations such as the Housing Corporation.

Fig. 1.17 Mass housing on slopes, Hong Kong (Photograph by Louise Cooke)

(*d*) To provide information and guidelines relevant to the valuation of land for future house building.

This book is therefore intended to be used by those whose work involves house design and site layout – town planners, architects, surveyors, engineers and others – and by those who need to be able to appreciate and assess the financial and other implications of house design and site layouts prepared by others. Local authority planners in development control, land buyers in all sectors and housing officers controlling subsidies all fall within this latter category. The contents of the book apply both before and after firm commitment of land acquisition and the granting of outline planning permission. A knowledge of house designs and possible site layouts will be essential in assessing the potential of sites under consideration, both in terms of a developer being able to cater for his/her intended market or, for example, a local authority planner wishing to see houses provided to an aesthetically high standard. Equally, the contents may apply at a later stage of preparing detailed plans and layouts by pooling ideas which have already been successfully used.

Chapter 2

Physical constraints and opportunities of sloping land

Ground slope and water table

A high water table causes problems of excavation, flooded services, basements and unstable foundations. It is indicated by test wells and a mottled soil. The height of the water table depends on precipitation and evapotranspiration and in most climates varies quite considerably, especially seasonally. There are therefore usually three zones to be recognized – permanent saturation, intermittent saturation and non-saturation. In areas of uniformly permeable bedrocks, these zones tend to follow topography in a rather subdued form (Fig. 2.1).

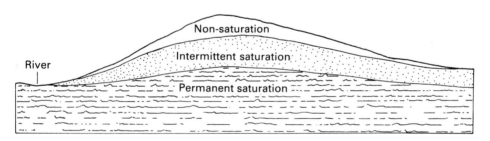

Fig. 2.1 Zones of saturation in uniformly permeable bedrocks tend to follow the topography

Watercourses are usually found where the zone of permanent saturation comes to the surface. The extent to which these zones are a subdued form of surface topography depends on the rate of water flow (permeability) of the rocks: the more permeable the rocks, the more subdued the water table. Thus a water table on clays would usually be closer in shape to the land surface than one for example on sandstone.

This assumes uniformly permeable bedrocks. Where permeable meets less permeable there can be various effects on water table. It may be brought to the surface in the form of a spring at the base of where the permeable layer meets the impermeable.

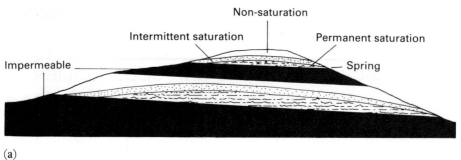

(a)

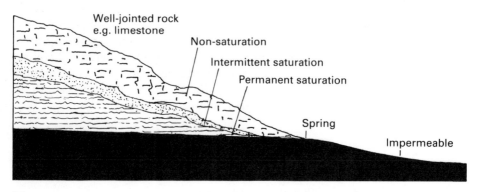

(b)

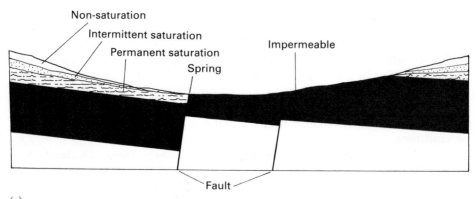

(c)

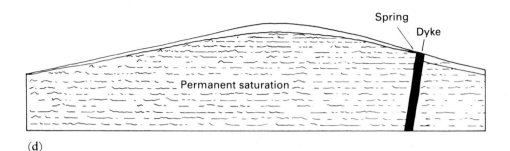

(d)

Fig. 2.2a, b, c, d Springs often result where permeable and impermeable strata come together

The height of the water table can have serious implications for site layouts of housing, particularly on the lower reaches of slopes or where an impermeable layer comes to the surface. The presence of a water table may also make land slippage more likely, particularly after disturbance of the natural groundslope by site works. Water in the subsoil increases its weight and also acts as a lubricant. Both of these factors tend to cause slippage. Generally, these obstacles to building on slopes can be overcome at extra cost by earthworks or drainage as explained in Chapter 5.

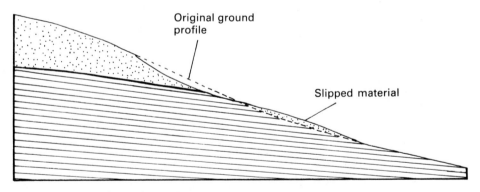

Fig. 2.3 A water table such as the junction of permeable and impermeable strata can encourage slippage.

Local climates on slopes

Large-scale steep slopes in mountainous regions have very different climates from those in surrounding lowlands. There are wide variations from one part of a slope to another according to the direction which the slope is facing. Upslope, air temperature tends to fall, there is higher rainfall, more snow, stronger winds,

17

higher humidity and more cloud. These, however, are only generalized trends and there are many local variations which do not conform.

In the kind of site in the UK where mass housing is likely to be built, some of these factors are unlikely to have much effect. They are really important only in a mountainous landscape. Nevertheless, there are climatic effects which can certainly be worth considering even on relatively gentle slopes as little as a few tens of metres in height. Sunlight and the amount of insolation received can vary a lot within an area large enough for only one house. On a slightly larger scale, wind can be very different from one part of a slope to another, both stronger and weaker than on the level, according to circumstances. Rainfall can be different from on-level sites and, with strong winds, can be near horizontal or even slightly upwards, a very important consideration in constructional design. Cold air drainage can lead to frost hollows even on quite modest, small-scale slopes.

Sunlight and insolation

Sunlight is regarded as beneficial for housing, especially in the UK, which is not over-blessed with it. This is because its adverse effects on human beings are easily controlled by opening windows or using blinds, though its damaging effects on furniture, carpets and other fittings should be taken into account where these are of special value.

In house design the important question concerning sunlight is its duration; for example, which part of the day or month does it shine and the direction and altitude of the sun.

On slopes, radiant energy exchanges are modified and local circulations sometimes develop, especially in valleys where there is little interference from pressure gradients covering large areas. Solar radiation on the ground is greatest on surfaces at right angles to the rays of the sun. Consequently, south-facing slopes receive more insolation than flat land; north-facing slopes less (all the following discussion refers to the northern hemisphere except where otherwise stated).

In fact, the amount of radiation received by the ground (not hours of sunshine) depends on five interacting variables: orientation of slope, angle of slope, latitude, time of day and time of year. For example, at latitude 50 °N the greatest intensity of radiation occurs at noon on slopes of 26.5° in mid-summer, 50° at the equinoxes and gradients of 72° in mid-winter. The angles of slope for maximum intensity of radiation are steeper for more northerly latitudes. The reverse trend is found on north-facing slopes – the steeper the slope the less radiation received. In fact, at 55 °N north-facing slopes of 11.5° or more, a little steeper than 1 in 5, receive no direct radiation at all in mid-winter. East-facing slopes receive maximum insolation in the morning with west-facing slopes in the afternoon. The gradient which receives maximum insolation is a flatter one in summer than the one which receives maximum insolation in winter for any latitude, though the angles at which maximum insolation is received does still depend on latitude.

Geiger (1965) relates direct insolation to angle and direction of slope, time of day and time of year. As might be expected, on gradients likely to be used for mass housing, the direction of slope is a more important determinant of direct radiation than the angle of slope. It is only on slopes with a northerly component that the angle is important.

K. Schütte (1943) has devised a simple method for calculating the amount of radiation falling on an air surface. The incident radiation on a slope can be calculated from one of two formulae:

1. *Slope facing into the sun*
   $$Is = (I \sin \alpha \cos \delta) + (I \cos \alpha \cos \gamma \sin \delta)$$

2. *Slope facing away from the sun*
   $$Is = (I \sin \alpha \cos \delta) - (I \cos \alpha \cos \gamma \sin \delta)$$

   where Is is the incident radiation (W/m^2)
   δ is the angle of slope
   α is the altitude of the sun
   γ is the slope–solar azimuth angle (angle between the solar azimuth angle and the normal to the slope)

Example: Intensity of solar radiation on a slope of 10° at 20° S of E at 3 p.m. on 21 October at 50 °N:
The declination of the sun is as follows:

21 March and 21 September	0°
21 February, 21 October, 21 April and 21 August	$11\frac{1}{2}°$
21 May, 21 July, 21 January and 21 November	$20\frac{1}{4}°$
21 December and 21 June	$23\frac{1}{2}°$

The declination on 21 October is 11.5°.
The hour angle for noon sun time plus 3 hours will be $3 \times 15° = 45°$

$$\begin{aligned} \sin \alpha &= (\sin 11.5° \times \sin 50°) + (\cos 11.5° \times \cos 50° \times \cos 45°) \\ &= (0.1994 \times 0.7660) + (0.9799 \times 0.6428 \times 0.7071) \\ &= 0.153 + 0.4454 \\ &= 0.5984 \end{aligned}$$

Solar altitude 36°45′
solar azimuth angle m is

$$\begin{aligned} \tan \epsilon &= \frac{\sin 45°}{(\sin 50° \times \cos 45°) - (\cos 50° \times \tan 11.5°)} \\ &= \frac{0.7071}{(0.7660 \times 0.7071) - (0.6428 \times 0.2035)} \\ &= 1.72 \end{aligned}$$

Therefore the solar azimuth angle is 59° 50′ W of S
or $\epsilon = 59° 50′ + 180° = 239° 50′$ SW of N
slope – solar azimuth angle = solar azimuth angle – 20° = 39° 50′.

The intensity of direct solar radiation normal to the sun may be taken as being approximately 800 W/m^2. The intensity of direct radiation on the slope facing the sun is

Is = $(I \sin \alpha \cos \delta) + (I \cos \alpha \cos \gamma \sin \delta)$
  = $(800 \sin 36° 45' \times \cos 10°) + (800 \cos 36° 45' \times \cos 39° 50' \times \sin 10°)$
  $(800 \times 0.5983 \times 0.9848) + (800 \times 0.8023 \times 0.7687 \times 0.1736)$
  = 560 W/m^2 (approximately)

The incident radiation on the slope of 10°, 20 °N of W at the same time, date and latitude is

Is = $(I \sin \alpha \cos \delta) - (I \cos \alpha \cos \gamma \sin \delta)$
  = $(800 \sin 36° 45' \times \cos 10°) - (800 \cos 36° 45' \times \cos 39° 50' \times \sin 10°)$
  $(800 \times 0.5983 \times 0.9848) - (800 \times 0.8023 \times 0.7687 \times 0.1736)$
  = 384 W/m^2 (approximately)

Using this formula in, for example, a computer program, a profile of incident radiation throughout the year on any given slope can be obtained.

There is evidence, however, to show that in mid-European latitudes more radiation is received indirectly than directly from the sun (Collmann 1958). This has the effect of evening out the radiation received on all slopes.

Where surfaces are frequently wet, perhaps as a result of dew, the warmest slopes are frequently south-west facing rather than south-facing. This is because some of the heat received in the forenoon is used to evaporate moisture from the ground, whilst that received in the afternoon is used to heat ground and buildings. Garnett (1939) gives an example at Kinlochleven (56° 50' N) where a south-facing slope of 25° has a potential insolation income of almost three times that of a north-facing slope of 30° in summer. Daylight, however, lasts about an hour longer on the north-facing slope. Crowe (1971) estimates that on average in mid-latitudes, a south-facing slope of 20° has similar insolation income as flat land 8° to 9° further south and that north-facing slope of 20° similar to flat land 12° to 15° further north.

Eighty per cent of the longwave radiation from a surface is directed towards the central 30° dome of the sky (Jones 1976). Slopes lose less net longwave radiation than level ground but Geiger (1965) estimates that this reduction is only 10 per cent on a slope of 30°, often less than the effects of cold air drainage downslope.

Bailey (1968), quoting F. Lanscher, in fact indicates the ratio of effective outgoing radiation for all angles of slope with those most likely to be encountered for mass housing being as follows:

angle of slope	0°	5°	10°	15°	20°	30°
effective outgoing radiation (%)	100	99.6	98.6	97.0	95.1	90.0

Local winds

These affect the rate of cooling, removal of pollution and transmission of sound.

Radiant energy exchanges can lead to the development of local winds on slopes and consequent effects on rainfall, especially where there is some enclosure as in a valley. The air above a slope in sunshine becomes warmer (and less dense) than the air at the same level above flat land because more insolation is received on all slopes in sunshine than is received in neighbouring flat land. A circulation develops with upslope anabatic winds, first on east-facing slopes. The strength of this depends on steepness of the slope and on the amount of radiation absorbed (Pedgley 1974). This circulation is very likely to be affected by surface roughness such as from housing. When moving, air acts rather like a viscous liquid and can surround objects such as housing to some extent in defiance of gravity.

The warm rising air cools adiabatically and subsiding air warms, so initial temperature differences diminish. Where the atmosphere is unstable, local showers may develop. In the same way as winds develop up a slope they can also develop up a valley with a downflow at night. They tend to occur later in the day than winds up a slope.

Fig. 2.4 Hemmed in by high moorlands to east and west, Darwen in Lancashire is an industrial town where caution may be necessary to avoid sites suffering from cold air drainage.

At night, air above slopes cools more than air at a similar level above flat ground due to less effective outgoing radiation. Cold air slips downslope (katabatic wind) and can be dammed up against obstacles such as houses, particularly if terraced. Winds of similar type but greater strength develop in valleys and tend to occur later in the night than downslope winds, continuing after sunrise.

A number of studies of daily temperature variations on slopes have been made, but few explicitly take into account the effects of housing. The temperature differences can be quite appreciable even in small valleys. For example, in the New Forest, Morris and Barry (1963) recorded a temperature difference of 2.3 °C between a valley bottom and ridge only 15.38 m different in height. In the Upper Irfon Valley, George (1963) recorded a temperature difference of 6.5 °C over a height difference of 211 m. Harrison (1967 and 1971) estimates that temperatures may increase as much as 0.17 °C per metre change in height over a range of 20 m or more, though the rate decreases for height differences of more than about 40 m.

Air temperatures in valleys in fact usually have a greater daily range than nearby level ground due to a high level of daytime insolation and cold air drainage at night. Near the top of a slope, on the other hand, the temperature variation will probably be less. Such locations may be cooled by stronger winds during the day and warmed as a result of cold air drainage away from the hill crest at night.

Locally cold air drainage can be a serious problem. Even a small obstacle such as a terrace of houses or even a hedge can dam cold air and lead to a frosty area. In fact, this principle is used in landscaping on slopes to divert cold air to where it will cause least harm and nuisance. To prevent damming and overflowing, hedges or belts of trees may be arranged to divert cold air (Fig. 2.5).

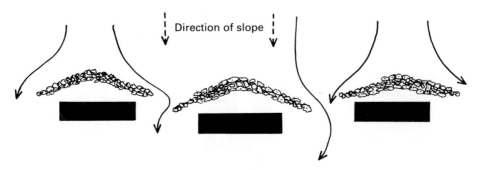

Fig. 2.5 Shelterbelts of hedges or trees to divert cold air drainage.

In industrial areas, cold air drainage can also result in pollution problems. With cold air occupying a valley floor, air-borne effluent being lighter than its surroundings will rise through the denser, colder air to a level where it meets warmer air above the inversion caused by the cold air drainage. Smoke and other pollutants may form a layer between cold and warm air and spread out horizontally to meet ground level part way up the valley side. Hillside housing at the junction of cold and warm air may well be persistently affected by pollution rising from below.

Valleys are also commonly prone to fog. It tends to collect on still nights. It checks the emission of heat but it may also prevent a considerable part of the next day's sunlight from reaching the ground.

In valleys, therefore, several levels may be prone to their own disadvantages. The lower reaches can be subject to cold air drainage and fog; further up there may be air pollution as a result of cold air drainage below and a temperature inversion and the highest parts are likely to experience the strongest winds. These are all dangers to be avoided or alleviated in the detailed design of housing sites.

What has been said so far applies to slopes when there are clear skies and weak pressure gradients in the area. Local circulations such as these can be prevented from becoming established by regional airflows. These airflows can, however, be appreciably modified locally by slopes. Gloyne (1964) estimates that on windward slopes no steeper than 20° to 30° and leeward slopes of up to 10°, air flows smoothly. Over steeper slopes, air does not follow the form of the slope but leaves unaffected areas which are larger on the leeward than on the windward side.

Wind speed is also affected by slope. Geiger (1965) estimates that an increase of 50–60 per cent in windspeed can occur on slopes of only 3°–10° on the windward side. On the leeward side a slope of between 2° and 10° can involve a speed reduction of 10–30 per cent. R E Lacy (1977) has estimated the windspeed effects of an isolated slope as a mean windspeed 10 m above a ridge which is 75 m above the surrounding area; this may be 50 per cent higher than 10 m above the surrounding plain when the wind is at right angles to the slope. Also, it is well known that precipitation is often different between windward and leeward sides. For an isolated hill, Geiger (1965) recorded 5–10 per cent more on the leeward side.

Olgyay (1963) also observed that where a hill is high enough to cause precipitation, the areas which have the lowest windspeeds have the most precipitation.

The combination of wind and rain – driving rain – has very important design and constructional implications. Wind travelling up a slope can carry rain near horizontal or even slightly upwards. As most buildings are designed for vertically falling rain, this clearly has serious effects. Lacy (1977) gives details of which parts of buildings are most likely to be exposed:

(a) When the wind blows at right angles to the roof ridge line there is suction just above the eaves on both windward and leeward sides, the latter as a result of an eddy behind the building. The suction and therefore damage caused is greatest for roofs with a pitch of less than 15°. It is virtually zero at 30°. Roofs with a pitch of 35° or more usually cause a sufficient obstruction for there to be a positive pressure on the windward side. In such cases there is a zone of suction near the ridge.

(b) When the wind is parallel to the ridge the windward sides of roofs of all pitches are affected.

(c) At the corners and along the edges of roofs and walls, vortices are caused by obliquely blowing winds rolling over the edges of the roof.

(d) Around projections such as chimney stacks which cause eddies in their wake.

(e) Immediately above overhangs in roofs, especially where there is a balcony below.

British Standards Institution Code of Practice CP 3: Ch 5 'Loading: Part 2 Wind Loads' (1972) uses a value of an additional 10 per cent design wind speed for the effects of exposed hill slopes or the funnelling effects of wind in a valley and a decrease of 10 per cent for steep-sided, enclosed and sheltered valleys:

$$Vs = V \times S_1 \times S_2 \times S_3$$

Vs is the design wind speed

V is the maximum gust speed for the locality presented by BSI (as above) in the form of a UK map

S_1 is the factor for local topography. Where there are no special effects this is taken as 1. For exposed hills rising well above surrounding countryside and valleys where there is a funnelling effect, it is 1.1. For an enclosed valley, a value of 0.9 may be used. More extreme values within the range 0.85 to 1.2 are sometimes used.

S_2 is the factor for roughness of the environment, gust duration and the height of the structure.

BSI Code of Practice CP 3 relates roughness of the environment, gust duration and height of structure. Where the structure is on or near to a steep slope, its effective height may be increased in accordance with French Code of Practice (Règles NV 65)

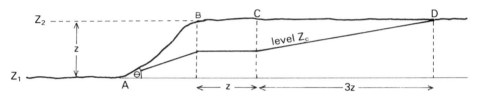

Fig. 2.6

In Fig. 2.6 Z_1 is the level at the foot of the hill
Z_2 is the level at the top of the hill
$Z_2 - Z_1 = z$
A is the intersection of level Z_1 with the slope
B is the intersection of level Z_2 with the slope
BC $= z$
CD $= 3z$
in front of A, $Z_c = Z_1$
from B to C_1, effective height level $Z_c = Z_1 + \dfrac{2 - \tan \theta_z}{1.7}$
behind D_1 $Z_c = Z_2$
where $\tan \theta \geqslant 2$
assume   in front of C, $Z_c = Z_1$
between C and D interpolate
behind D, $Z_c = Z_2$

S is the factor for the design life of the building. Normally this is taken as the probability that the value will be exceeded only once in 50 years (0.02 probability in any one year or 0.63 probability that it will be exceeded at least once in any period of 50 years). In these cases $S_3 = 1$. S_3 values for more stringent standards are explained in Lacy (1977) p 89.

Shelter

For houses which have to be built in windy locations there are two main groups of possible ways to reduce the ill-effects: by designing the shape of the house envelope to fit with the natural air currents and give shelter to outdoor space most used by residents and, secondly, by building some form of windbreak such as a hedge, shelterbelt, an artificial screen, wall or by earthworks. A review of the possibilities is contained in Abbott and Pollit (1980), which are more applicable to one-off designs rather than mass housing.

For mass housing the possibilities will be limited by the amount of land available. Modification of natural air currents often results in rather low densities for the housing. Also, mass housing is less likely to be built in the climatically extreme sites than is individual housing.

However, there are several design possibilities for improving the environment around mass housing, some of which rely on taking advantage of natural shelter, modified house design or the design of landscaped areas which would previously have been used as open space regardless of local climatic conditions (Fig. 2.7).

House design
The shape of the house envelop can be modified to fit in with the natural airflows, aided by earthworks or windbreaks (Fig. 2.7).

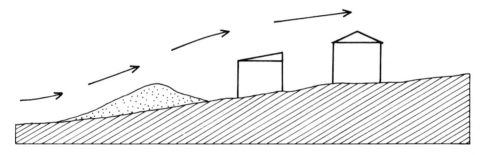

Fig. 2.7 Contours and dwelling shape can be moulded to fit natural contours.

There will be many variations on this general principle which can be worked out individually for specific sites. Olgyay (1963), Halprin (1971), Evans (1957) and Lawson (1968) give advice for those embarking on site layouts in such situations.

Windbreaks
Hedges and artificial screens are among the most practical form of shelter on most mass housing sites. There are many arrangements which can be used on slopes (and on level ground) to divert cold air drainage and/or to block wind funnels (Fig. 2.9). Lynch (1971) estimates that thick belts of trees reduce wind velocities by more than 50 per cent for a distance downwind of ten times their height and by 35 per cent for a distance of twenty times their height. He recommends that belts should be 15.25 m to 43.75 m deep and should rise gradually in height on the windward side to reduce air turbulence on the lee. An open structure also reduces turbulence.

Screens and hedges around the gardens of housing estates of medium and high density may be quite sufficient. However, it is quite common for developers to take the opposite view: that on exposed estates the fencing should be open or palisade type to allow the wind to penetrate, otherwise it is more likely to be blown down! At lower densities, extra screens may be desirable, linking buildings to perimeter fences to prevent a funnelling effect around detached houses or between pairs of semi-detached.

Caborn (1965) gives some more examples and Beddall (1950) and Jensen (1954) give advice on construction. Jensen examined various types of artificial screen and came to the conclusion that screens consisting of 35–40 per cent holes give the greatest shelter. Blenk and Trienes (1956) put it slightly higher at 40–50 per cent.

Fig. 2.8 Topography as dramatic as the cliffs at Dover will have an important effect on local climate.

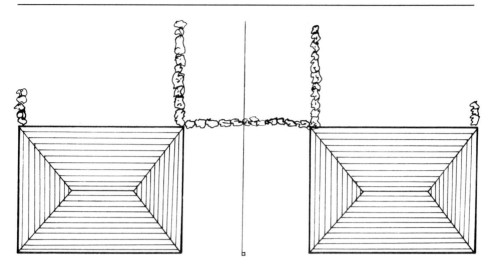

Fig. 2.9 Windbreaks can be formed in various ways.

Earthworks
Low banking around a group of houses can have a significant effect in giving wind shelter and often this can be made to fit in with other landscaping and open space arrangements. This has particular potential if a natural or artificial hollow already exists to accommodate the houses and, if carefully placed, earthworks can also assist cold air drainage away from the houses. This kind of arrangement however is possible only where a large amount of open space is to be provided. There is also a problem in that the positioning of earthworks is effective only over a range of windspeeds; without research it is hazardous to estimate the actual windspeeds.

Trees
Tree planting is perhaps a less likely proposition than earthworks or screens for most mass housing developments. They require a relatively large amount of land to be effective (though it is quite possible to site new housing to take advantage of existing trees). Also it takes some time for them to become a useful shelter. The Ministry of Agriculture, Fisheries and Food has observed some beneficial effects after five or six years (Ministry of Agriculture, Fisheries and Food 1968). Planted close to housing they can, of course, block off too much light (Abbott and Pollit 1980, pp 237–8) or even cause damage to foundations.

Cadman (1963) describes the sheltering effect of a tree belt. Wind speed is reduced to 80–90 per cent of its unobstructed speed up to a distance of 20 times the height of the windbreak behind it. It should be remembered however that shelter will cause an increase in windspeed elsewhere around the margins of the shelter due to a funnelling effect. It is also possible that the first few feet of shelter above ground level will be more penetrable than the higher parts sheltered by branches, so the shelter may be lost in the very parts where it is most needed.

Also, of course, with deciduous trees some of the shelter effect is lost in winter, the time when it is most likely to be needed. Jensen (1954) estimates this loss at about 40 per cent.

The Ministry of Agriculture, Fisheries and Food (1968) also estimates that the lengths of the most effective wind breaks are at least twelve times their height for winds at right angles to them and correspondingly longer for winds at less than 90°; for example, twenty-four times at 45°.

Abbott and Pollit (1980: 292–5) give a list of species suitable for shelter.

Soil types

This section is concerned with soil composition. Earth movements are discussed in Chapter 5. Soil composition is of relevance to house construction in so far as it affects foundation design and the construction of roads and other ancillary works. Bedrock, vegetation and climate, all of which are affected by slope, as well as topography are important in affecting soil composition. Position on a slope affects the thickness of the soil which generally becomes thinner with increasing height, and also affects the thickness of constituent layers or horizons. The washing out of chemicals will also affect soil composition, though how this is sufficient to influence choice of foundation is uncertain. When building it is of more practical significance to remember that soil composition and depth is likely to vary according to height on slope and this should be considered when choosing where to take test boreholes. The relationship of soil to topography is treated in detail by Bunting (1967, Ch. 6).

Soil composition can also give an indication of drainage conditions. Where drainage is impeded the soil is always paler than freely drained similar soil. It is often mottled or brownish yellow in colour due to the presence of hydrated oxides of iron such as limonite or bluish-grey or olive due to ferrous compounds. These are sticky, structureless and compact when wet, mottled and rust coloured when dry. Frequently these compounds occur as concretions which may coalesce to form a continuous layer or pan. The depth of these characteristics gives an indication of the extent of waterlogging. Another sign of waterlogging is where the channels of living roots are lighter in colour than their surroundings. This is a result of roots taking away oxygen, thereby impoverishing the soil, making it lighter in colour. Details of the variety of forms that these characteristics can take are contained in Bunting (1967, especially Ch. 11). Soil sampling techniques are explained in Clarke (1957) and Brade-Birks (1946).

When examining soil types for a given site, much useful information can be gained from geological maps, local records; and where development has been carried out on adjacent sites, reference can be made to the department administering the Building Regulations. Other useful sources of documentation are explained in Hodgkinson (1981a). These will give a general indication of the prevailing soil type and a guide to the type of foundation likely to be required. It should be noted that, particularly on large sites, soil composition is liable to vary a lot and only a thorough site investigation will reveal these variations. Areas of fill may also be identified from local records. However, details of the nature and bearing capacity of fill are rarely kept and more detailed testing will be essential where this is suspected.

The traditional 'shallow' foundation for domestic building has been the simple, non-reinforced concrete strip cast at a suitable bearing level. Brickwork built off this to damp proof course level must be selected to withstand moisture, frost and chemical action. High labour costs and the increased use of mechanical diggers and ready-mixed concrete now makes mass concrete trenchfill footings a cost-effective option, especially where foundation layout is straightforward. These footings are also most economic in firm, shrinkable clays where the depth required to overcome changes in moisture content is greater than in granular soils, and where traditional strips are difficult to construct. Care must be taken with trenchfill footings to allow for incoming and outgoing service connections: it is an expensive process to cut holes in hard, mass concrete!

For housing on slight to medium slopes, i.e. up to gradients of about 5° (1 in 11) where the site has been graded and terraced to form a series of flat platforms, simple raft foundations can be an economic solution. This is sometimes the favoured method in large private developments where relatively low densities (below about 150 bedspaces per hectare) allow such use of the site or where savings gained by using standard house types above a prepared substructure can offset the additional cost of engineered reinforced foundations.

The minimum allowable specifications for substructure according to soil composition are laid down in the UK Building Regulations 1976 (D7).

Rock

Included in this section are sandstones, limestones, shales, igneous rocks and hard solid chalk, which are hard, rigid and strongly cemented materials and usually require only levelling and the cavities filling. Most are relatively impermeable and stable except where used in thin layers or weathered. Usually they are of very good load-bearing capacity with little or no settlement. Chalk may be subject to frost damage and limestone may contain 'swallow holes'.

Foundations are generally shallow wide strip (below the frost zone in the case of chalk). Additional costs are unlikely except where the rock has been quarried and the backfill is poor. In such cases, raft foundations may be appropriate at extra cost.

Non-cohesive soils

Compact gravels and sands

These are permeable, moderately compressible and easily excavated. They have good load-bearing capacity with minimal settlement. The bearing capacity may be reduced if submerged. Also, they may be affected by vibration. Removal of

29

subsoil water from excavations is always expensive and therefore foundations on permeable soils should be kept above the water table.

Wide strip foundations are usually satisfactory but raft or deep piles may be necessary to overcome water on vibration problems.

Loose or fine gravel and sand
These are generally permeable, moderately compressible and easily excavated, and more subject to water and frost. Sands and gravels which are 'clean' (containing less than about 10–12 per cent silt or clay) can cause problems for house construction without stabilization. A greater proportion of silt or clay is better for house construction though all are suitable for road building.

A simple test for the proportion of silt or clay in a sandy or gravel soil is simply to spread out a sample and inspect the proportion of soil which is composed of visible particles like sand or gravel compared to fine dust such as silt or clay. If this proves difficult, the clay and silt fraction may be washed off by shaking a sample of the soil in water repeatedly until the water is clear. Dry weights before and after washing can then be compared.

There may be extra costs for foundations which may be strip, pile or raft, depending on conditions, especially water content.

Cohesive soils

Dry compact clays
These are generally stable. There is, however, often a substantial settlement period due to the lengthy process of squeezing water out from the pores due to compressibility. They generally have good load-bearing capacity but are less permeable than non-cohesive soils. They are often affected by seasonal shrinkage and proximity to trees, which may influence site layout (Campling 1980; Reynolds 1979; BS 5837: 1980).

Foundations are usually wide or deep strip. The additional costs are usually marginal except where the clays vary over the site.

Silty and other highly shrinkable clays
These are unpredictable due to their impermeable and unstable state, and the effects of seasonal shrinkage and trees. Silt is particularly susceptible to frost and heaves badly. It is also very unstable when wet. Plastic or shrinkable clays and silts are therefore much more difficult for both house and road construction than are non-plastic or dry compact clays and silts. The two groups may be distinguished from each other by adding a small amount of water to a sample of the soil so that it can be moulded without sticking to the hands. It is then rolled out to about an eighth of an inch in diameter and then reworked into a ball. If this can be done without cracking, it is a plastic shrinkable clay. If it can be remoulded into a ball but the ball cracks when worked again, it is a non-plastic clay. If it cannot be remoulded into a ball, it is a plastic silt or an organic soil. If it

would not even roll out into a thread, it is a non-plastic silt. Plastic clays can also be recognized by their soapy feel and because they form a hard crust when moulded and dried.

There are usually substantial additional costs for deep strip, pile, beam or raft foundations. Short bore piles (4–5 m) will probably be most economical on depths of more than 1.5 m (Hodgkinson 1981b). They also have the advantage that piling can take place in winter when trenches for strips may be waterlogged or damaged by frost. Building near trees is a particular danger on shrinkable clays but can be possible with pile-bored foundations. Where trees have been removed it will take at least five years before the moisture content stabilizes. Piles can be used taking into account uplift in swelling clays. Close to water courses, clays may have a firm shrunken crust. Raft foundations will reduce the tendency to squeeze out the underlying layer (*BRE Digest* 67, 1966).

Peat

Organic deposits such as peat do not have sufficient bearing capacity to be considered as a base for foundations and can entail excessive pile foundations extended to a safe bearing stratum. Additional cost will depend on the thickness of the organic stratum. For example, at Thamesmead the piles extended 14 m from the surface through 10 m of peat to a safe-bearing soil. Reinforced rafts are sometimes used.

Fill

The foundations necessary and additional costs vary greatly according to method and standard of laying, type of material, extent of compaction and period since laying (see for example Hodgkinson 1981a).

Properly graded and compacted permeable fill can be stable with only moderate compressibility and good load-bearing capacity. Wide or deep strips can be used with no additional costs. However, poor natural compaction of fills which have been badly placed can mean that normal strip foundations would be inadvisable as the process may take 10 to 20 years to complete. In general, uneven settlement is the greatest problem due to irregularities in density and moisture content; this problem may be exacerbated on waste disposal and sanitary land where fills suffer organic decomposition or physio-chemical breakdown which could produce potentially explosive substances and gases such as hydrogen sulphide and methane. Special investigation of badly placed fills is essential. The foundation types are variable but reinforced deep strips are most likely or, where a good bearing crust overlays fill, rafts.

A large housing authority such as the City of Birmingham uses rafts for the greater part of its domestic building. Much recent housing has been in redevelopment areas where previous buildings, some containing basements, conceal ground conditions which are difficult to assess. In such instances the higher apparent cost of raft substructures over traditional footings and slabs can often be saved. Less time is needed for accurate surveys and expensive individual adjustments both in design, on site and filling and compacting poor ground can be eliminated.

Ashes and industrial waste may contain sulphates which attack ordinary concrete. In such cases, sulphate-resisting cement must be used for concrete and mortars below ground, although expert advice should be sought if high concentrations are suspected. Specially designed reinforced piles are likely to be needed.

Chapter 3

Site planning for housing on slopes

The physical background to house building on slopes was the subject of the previous chapter. We now go on to look at the special considerations which should be a part of designing the configuration of buildings, spaces and communications to foster, or at least enable, activities on sloping sites. This chapter makes no attempt to be a comprehensive guide to site planning. It merely picks out for the designer's consideration some of the factors which are specific to mass housing on slopes.

Site planning is intricately linked to house design. There is some arbitrariness in the division of material between this chapter and the next. Distances between buildings, enclosure of spaces, experiences of massing, orientation of buildings and many other features of house design can all affect the layout of the site and vice versa. This is not always the case, however. The decision for example, on whether to overcome slope by cut-and-fill or a split level house form may usually be taken quite independently of site layout. Those features of house design which are influenced by site layout are introduced in this chapter and are dealt with more fully along with other house design features less influenced by layout in the next chapter. Here we consider house design primarily from the point of view of the planner, while the next chapter includes site planning from the point of view of the house designer.

Initial approaches to design and layout

The relationship between a building, its site and setting is fundamental to planning and architectural design. As buildings are primarily a means of sheltering human activity from the elements, the history of architecture could be presented as a movement from caves, tree houses and other natural shelters in which the link between inhabitants and their natural environment is immediate, to space-inspired technology where the two are entirely separate and the only 'shelter' is a personal life-support system. Less dramatically, it can be appreciated that the more the construction industry relies on standard design solutions made up from factory components divorced from a given location, the more difficult it is to tailor an individual building to a particular site. It is especially difficult if the site is sloping.

Apart from any psychological necessity for housing to have a sense of place or personal identity (aspects which many recent schemes have tended to ignore to their disadvantage), it is not easy for a developer to impose a standardized layout on a sloping site. This does not mean that only highly personalized and individualistic solutions are acceptable. Indeed, the revival of 'vernacular' forms, if applied thoughtlessly, can be just as bland as any more brutal and regimented design. It does mean, however, that when a designer encounters a sloping site all the issues concerning the juxtaposition of land form and building need careful attention and thorough resolution.

Once a site has been earmarked for housing, there are three principal ways in which planners and architects can react to any slope:

1. *Site inspired.* The layout including access to, position and orientation of dwellings can be considered as a direct product of the slope, allowing the overall design to take its inspiration from the setting.

2. *Land-form adapted.* The land forms can be artificially manipulated to make construction easier. This method includes the creation of terraced areas on to which 'flat site' designs can be placed.

3. *Special dwellings.* Special house designs can be used, the choice depending on the degree of slope, orientation and place within the overall layout.

Site inspired
The historic hill town is perhaps the most obvious example of this type: means of access and dwelling-form evolve organically from the topography, often without recourse to any particular architectural gymnastics (Figs 3.1 to 3.5). Recent examples which follow this approach are the student housing at the University of Surrey on the slopes beneath Guildford Cathedral (architects Maguire and Murray), the small layout on the slopes of Kingstanding Beacon for the City of Birmingham designed by the Live Project Department of the Birmingham School of Architecture (Fig. 3.6) and the low rise development in Basildon designed under the direction of Clive Plumb. A less dramatic but thoughful and economic approach is being built by W Timms and Son under the direction of Charter Design at Banbury (see below).

Land-form adapted
Site adaptation is the most popular means of overcoming slopes of less than about 7° (1 in 8). It is especially favoured by large organizations in the private sector and small local authorities; developers who use a variety of standard shell designs and then alter the land form to accommodate them. Unless the principle of 'houses built on stilts' above the slope is adopted, some land adaptation will be necessary. There are many examples, too numerous for individual identification. The critical point for the designer, when this whole approach must be questioned, arises

when major earthworks and means of retention are necessary; for example, there are often problems of bringing vehicles on to the site.

Special designs

Where gradients are steeper than about 8° (1 in 7) it is more difficult to place flat site house designs upon them. Acknowledging the difficulty by planning the layout parallel to the contours or using shallow depth plan types (method 1) above) can overcome some problems, but often it will be necessary to design special forms to fit the slope. The redevelopment of steep gradients in the St Ann's District of Nottingham, Lambeth's Central Hill and the more suburban area of Frankley in Birmingham all employ the method of stepping floors down

Fig. 3.1 In an historic hill town (Granada, Spain) houses 'grow' organically from the natural slopes.

35

the slope within a single envelope. The redevelopment of the Byker area of Newcastle upon Tyne (designed by Ralph Erskine) uses long, flat blocks to step down the hillside and contrasts with nineteenth-century terraces on the same slope (Fig. 3.7). At Parkhill, close to the centre of Sheffield, the City Architect adapted deck access flats to the steeply sloping valley. By clever use of the hillside allied with an ingenious cross-section and snaking plan form all but one entry level of these flats (which are in a slab block structure rising to eleven storeys) has direct access to natural ground level without using steps or ramps.

In many of these specially designed structures the distinction between individual dwellings and flats is often tenuous. With more typical types of multi-storey housing, the problem of sloping land is less acute, affecting mainly the designs of the foundations and means of access to the lowest storey. Multi-storey can indeed be one of the more economical approaches to mass housing on steep slopes. This is a solution much used in a number of countries. In Sweden for example social and environmental factors as well as economics tend to encourage flats in the inner suburbs. The severe winters, the rocky terrain and large subsidies for public transport in some areas (including Stockholm) and opportunities for second homes on a large scale as well as the need to build on slopes, all favour building flats.

None of the three methods identified is mutually exclusive. Many layouts on sloping sites will employ at least two of these ways of overcoming or exploiting the particular situation. The pragmatic approach of some earlier builders can even be seen to use all three methods within the one solution. At Hebden Bridge in West Yorkshire, nineteenth-century housing is built in long rows along the steep sides

Fig. 3.2 Bridgnorth is an ancient settlement, climbing an escarpment above the River Severn. Without an imposed order to its plan, the houses cluster naturally up the slopes

Fig. 3.3 Access to housing in Bridgnorth is gained either off steep, curving streets . . .

Fig. 3.4 . . . cut up the hillside, sometimes passing under other dwellings

Fig. 3.5 . . . or off stepped alleyways

of the valley. Narrow terraces have been cut out and housing placed along them with the main access road running diagonally up the contour to reduce its gradient. Such is the steepness of the slope that at the lower level the buildings are five storeys high; on the upper level, only three. In fact, these are individual houses of two and three storeys built one directly above the other, each with direct access to its 'ground' floor.

Topography and related geology, hydrology, local climate and soils all

Fig. 3.6 These patio houses designed within the former Live Project Department at the Birmingham School of Architecture were an attempt to create a high-density, low-rise scheme with privacy on a particularly difficult hillside site (Kingstanding, Birmingham)

influence site layouts (and vice versa to some extent). Site layouts and the design of buildings, spaces and communications are closely inter-related. Nevertheless, neither site plan nor building, space or communication design follow from each other or from topography. There is no such thing as a correct site plan or house design. Choice of layout and design depend on who they are for, on demands and needs, set within constraints imposed by the physical features of the site and technological possibilities. Also, requirements may change as time passes. House extension or garages may be desired and these changes must not be forgotten in the initial layout.

Both house design and site planning are quite rightly influenced by local requirements and particular local landscapes. To some extent a design guide for housing on slopes should be of local application. Density, house styles, site requirements within the curtilage and even taste do not permit rigid guidance of world wide or even national application. Many parts of the USA and Australia for example have their own guides tailor-made for a particular local terrain (see for example Scott and Furphy 1979). Nevertheless, there are principles which are worthy of some general consideration and it is these which concern us here.

The configuration of land uses and activities

Generally, the steeper the slope and the more irregular in plan and section, the more it will influence the basic arrangement of the plan. Sites of irregular and

Fig. 3.7 The recent housing development at Byker, Newcastle upon Tyne (right) contrasts with the nineteenth-century terraces (left). Both forms step down the slope.

Fig. 3.8 Even at high density the rugged natural terrain gives a beautiful setting to many parts of Stockholm

steep topography often do not permit an intricate layout of closely related parts, only one quite simple in form, often based on the sub-division of the site into more comprehensible parts. Any geometry in the layout is usually best confined to these parts rather than the whole.

Spaces often create a problem on slopes. Many of the layouts successful on flat land are not at all satisfactory on slopes where the sides tend to become dissociated from each other. Thus the rectangular close is very difficult to achieve satisfactorily on a steep, even slope. Undulating land however gives many opportunities for enclosure. A loop pattern enclosing open space on the highest part is often successful. One such scheme is that at Walnut Creek, California, referred to in the next chapter.

Fig. 3.9 Hebden Bridge, Yorkshire: nineteenth-century terraces of houses are squeezed on to extremely steep valley sides whilst industry tends to concentrate on the very limited amount of flatter land on the valley floor.

For a hilltop of smaller dimensions, one possible solution is a central access road surrounded by rings of dwellings. At Harlow (Bishopsfield) a central service road enters beneath a single storey platform round the crown of a hill with covered parking and storage space. The platform carries a pedestrian concourse giving access to a ring of flats surrounding it. From here, footpaths sufficient for tradesmen's delivery floats run down the hillside giving access to a semi-circle of patio houses (Neylan 1966).

There are, however, exceptions to the generalization that sub-division of a hilly site into comprehensible parts is usually the best solution. The vision of the re-design for Rome of Pope Sixtus V is a glorious exception (Bacon 1974, pp 131–61). The problem of achieving a coherent design in this city of seven hills

41

Fig. 3.10 The rugged hill top makes a natural centre piece for this housing scheme in Stockholm

is a formidable one. Long straight ways ascend and descend with a rhythm which could have been lost had their direction been compromised by topography, a design enabled by the soft, rounded contours.

Treatment of the skyline is an important consideration on sloping sites. Low density housing usually results in a ragged, angular appearance (sky-line development). Where the housing can be brought together, on the other hand, it can add to the drama of the landscape by emphasizing relief. Planting is sometimes used to emphasize topography.

Housing layouts imply decisions on who is to get the best views, the distribution of daylight and sunlight and the configuration of public and private space. Gradients for public space, views obtainable and the daily and seasonal distribution of sunlight all influence its use. Often, too much open space is simply grassed over, a cheap initial solution but one with substantial maintenance costs and giving little benefit to residents.

Spaces may be designed so as to give some shade in summer and allow the sun to penetrate as much as possible in winter. This can be sought through the positioning, orientation and height of buildings. Deciduous trees can also help to achieve this. Attention should also be given to the albedo of walls and other structures facing the sun. These can have a substantial effect on the microclimate of intervening spaces as well as the heating of the buildings themselves.

It is important to design in terms of activities as well as spaces and buildings:

(a) Which parts of the sites will be used by children for playing? How will this be

Fig. 3.11 In classically-planned Bath, these houses step confidently up the slope, imposing a simple order and rhythm

    influenced by gradient? Will safety be affected?   for example by balls rolling off the site into a nearby road? How will the children get there?

(b) How will the disabled, elderly and mothers/fathers with prams move about?

(c) Will any of the steeper paths or stairs be especially treacherous when covered with snow? Will they be attractive to children playing?

(d) Which parts of the site will be attractive for people to congregate because of micro-climate, view or being a focus of activities? It is a waste of the potential of the site to allow roads and footpaths to become visual corridors. Spaces should be allowed to make the most of views possible from the site, usually the high points.

Fig. 3.12 These crescents in Bath curve sinuously around the contours, in contrast to those straight streets which cut across the natural slope

Fig. 3.13 Lansdown Crescent follows a series of curves, enclosing a grassy slope and taking advantage of south-facing rows over the city of Bath

Fig. 3.14 Does this add drama to the relief? Färsta, Stockholm

Fig. 3.15 Space left over planning; even children cannot find a use for it when steeply sloping. Pedestrians just want to get across it as quickly as possible rather than by the official route. Harborne, Birmingham

Fig. 3.16 Left-over space: The steeper the slope the more it becomes a barrier. Burnley, Lancashire

Fig. 3.17 Some enclosure may be achieved by planning around a taller building. Woodgate Valley, Birmingham

Fig. 3.18 Open space created on slopes is not often attractive to children because of its unsuitability for ball games. Planners should always ask themselves what they expect a site to be used for. Blackburn, Lancashire

Fig. 3.19 Circulation for pedestrians, particularly during the ice and snow of winter, is usually a problem on sloping sites. Building along the contours has resulted in only short lengths of footpaths and roads having steep gradients, but many residents use steps such as these to reach the shops. Frankley, Birmingham

47

Fig. 3.20 Spaces should always be planned to make the most of views from them, usually from high points.

Across or along the contours?

Some would regard building or roads along the contours as being more harmonious and more pleasing, if less dramatic, than structures against the contours. Building with the contours gives an opportunity to screen undesirable features such as roads by sinking them into the ground. It also gives better views from the housing and less steep road gradients, though possibly at the expense of greater lengths of roads and steep driveways to the houses. Sometimes where there is a steep cross-slope the street scene can have a lop-sided appearance, though this can be reduced to some extent by dissociating the buildings from the road visually. In fact, this can be used to advantage, for example, by achieving separation of vehicles and pedestrians.

Fig. 3.21 Inclines can help separation of pedestrians from traffic. As well as improving the environment for pedestrians, separation of the footpath reduces the width of the visual plane centred on the carriageway and is more in sympathy with the natural ground levels. Blackburn, Lancashire

Also, where there are buildings of various storey heights, slopes can help achieve enclosure by allowing land slope to compensate for variation in building height.

Appearance of the street scene is usually enhanced by separating the footpath from the carriageway. This reduces the width of the horizontal plane centred on the carriageway and is more in sympathy with the natural ground form. It also results in grass verges being less steep. The appearance may be even better if the carriageway is placed off-centre with planting on the wider verge to increase visual dissociation. On very steep slopes, flat roofs may be considered to improve the view downslope.

Roads diagonal to the slope often combine the disadvantages of those parallel and perpendicular to the slope. Gardens have awkward cross-slopes and house designs become complicated and expensive.

Layouts with roads parallel to the slope are also usually cheaper. If the slope occurs along the longer walls of the houses (usually back to front) the extra costs will be greater than if it is along the shorter walls (usually the frontage). However, 'long' and 'short' are not the same as 'side' and 'front'. For a house of given dimensions on sloping land it is not just a question of whether the long wall or the short wall is across the slope. If the long wall is the frontage there will be a shorter party wall and the arrangements and lengths of retaining walls will be different from the case where the long wall is along the side of the house. For two dwelling types from the National Building Agency's metric house shells (Numbers 9 and

Fig. 3.22 Although on a considerable incline of about 7° (1 in 8), enclosure has been maintained by keeping the spaces fairly narrow and sinking the footpath on both sides. The seating on a slightly less steep part of the site acts as a focal point. Darwen, Lancashire

Fig. 3.23 The simple courtyard plan on this estate in Cwmbran, Gwent, is disrupted by the effect of a cross-fall: an inappropriate layout for a sloping site.

Fig. 3.24 Not much enclosure in this square at Stourbridge, West Midlands. Few of the houses seem to take advantage of the long distance view northwards

27) Trickey (1975) calculated the following cost indices per dwelling in terraces of six:

Metric plan	Level ground	Slope 1: 10 parallel across	Slope 1: 6 parallel across
9	100.0	101.3 102.1	102.2 103.6
27	104.6	105.7 107.3	106.6 109.6

For a wide house type (8.62 m frontage, 5.81 m depth) the following extranormal substructure costs can be calculated from Gee (1962), graph 6:

	1:25	1:20	1:15	1:10	1:9	1:8	1:7	1:6	1:5
Slope across frontage	123	131	142	164	170	182	196	218	247
Slope front to back	109	112	118	132	137	146	161	182	213

For narrower house types, the extranormal costs for side slopes may be greater than this. Gee (1962) has calculated the following extra costs for brickwork in external walls up to the damp proof course in houses with a 1: 10 side slope as:

6.10 m depth × 9.15 m frontage	53% more than flat site
6.71 m depth × 9.15 m frontage	55% more than flat site
7.62 m depth × 9.15 m frontage	62% more than flat site

All these figures refer to the percentage of substructure costs on level ground. Using data from the National Building Agency (1976) it is possible to put these costs into perspective:

Cost breakdown for a typical private sector house outside London as at April 1976 (%)

Services	12	External works	7
Finishes	11	Site development	8
Superstructure	32	Professional fees	4
Substructure	7	Land and legal costs	19

For public sector housing less is spent on land and possibly external works, though the following categories from the Development Management Working Group (1978) are not comparable in all cases:

	London (%)	Rest of England and Wales (%)
Construction of dwelling	54	66
Land	19	10
Site development works	4	8
Professional services	5	7
Interest on land	9	4
Interest on building in progress	9	5

It seems possible that full costs according to slope may be rather higher than Gee's figures. As will be seen below, superstructure costs, external works, site development and services are all affected by land slope.

Therefore, in designing layouts for housing on slopes, one consideration will usually be to try to arrange the long walls along rather than across the contours, in so far as the savings in cost are not outweighed by any decrease in density or longer services and roads. For detached and semi-detached houses the long wall refers to the individual dwelling; for terraced housing it is usually the whole terrace which is orientated along the slope irrespective of the frontage to depth ratio of individual dwellings. This is because the cost effects of slope are greater on external walls than on party walls; also, if the terrace is positioned against the slope there will be the need for some external walling between the houses if the terrace is stepped, or a longer roof and extra external walling on the front and back if it is not stepped. The extra costs due to steps will obviously depend on the depth of the dwelling and other design factors, and the displacement of the step.

Fig. 3.25 When building across the contours, an unbroken ridge line is common in older terraces. Before the dormers, such a terrace must have had a much less angular appearance than its modern counterpart.
Rawtenstall, Lancashire

(a)

(b)   (c)

Fig. 3.26a, b Cut-and-fill along the contours with massive retaining wall on a very steep slope of about 25° (1 in 2). Road access zig-zags up the hillside. Rossendale, Lancashire

Fig. 3.26c The backs of the same houses. Rossendale, Lancashire

(a)

(b)

Fig.3.27a, b Housing solutions in the Woodgate Valley, Birmingham. (a) The public sector terraces along the contours contrast sharply with (b) the cut-and-fill solution with flat site houses of the private sector

However, figures from Davis, Belfield and Everest (1978) suggest that for a 1 m step, extra costs may be in the range of 7.5–8.2 per cent for single-storey housing, 5.4–6.2 per cent for two-storey housing and 4.5–4.7 per cent for three-storey housing.

Crawley (Broadfield 5)
Messrs Phippen Randall and Parkes, Architects of East Molesey, Surrey, have designed for the Guinness Trust at Broadfield 5, Crawley, a scheme consisting of 395 dwelling units at a gross density of 158 habitable rooms to the acre (*Housing Review* July/Aug. 1982, pp 127–9). Included is a single-person complex of 40 bedsitters and 8 two-person flatlets, 37 old people's flats and 63 other one and

two-person flats. Most of the other dwellings are two-and three-bedroom terraced houses.

Basically the scheme consists of a perimeter ring of houses with sixteen courts of housing and a few groups of infill housing within the site. About one third of the site is a north-facing slope varying in gradient between about 14° and 8° (1 in 4 to 1 in 7). Here, broad frontage, narrow depth two-storey houses have been built along the contours, mostly in short terraces of about four houses with parking courts enclosed between the terraces. In some cases, two-storey flats have been added to one or both ends of a pair of terraces to form an enclosed court. The southerly units of each court are south-facing garden entry types designed to take advantage of aspect and to avoid overlooking. Most of the houses are single aspect to avoid overlooking and to take advantage of the sunlight available.

The perimeter terraced housing runs across the contours and a conscious attempt has been made to keep the terrace as straight as possible, especially where they are stepped. The architects report that they have found split level housing uneconomic when car ports and garages cannot be included in publicly financed housing. The Broadfield scheme is a response by running short terraces along the contours and accepting changes of level between houses. Steps of 450–600 mm have proved to be most economical and this has determined the number of changes of level in a terrace. They have found that changes of level greater than this involve expensive retaining walls and external works while smaller steps incur expense on flashings and abutment details more frequently than is necessary.

Arden Estate, Banbury

Although the larger private developers and the smaller local authorities appear reluctant to adapt layouts and house types to cater for sloping sites, there are some notable exceptions. A recent scheme for Cherwell District Council by W Timms and Son (Builders) Ltd, and the Charter Design Group of Bedford is on an awkward site, yet it promises to provide attractively grouped and inexpensive houses aimed specifically at the first-time buyer (W Timms and Son (Builders Ltd 1981). The site is on the northern outskirts of Banbury and the estate will cover approximately 3.5 hectares on a north-east facing slope; an extension of a large Council development.

The scheme is a 'partnership development' with the Local Authority who will give priority to purchasers from the housing waiting list and other selected categories. The developer has thus been cushioned from the uncertainties of total speculation, and as the land was offered at discounted value it has been possible to produce a design-conscious scheme to sell at extremely competitive prices.

The architects initially tested the practicability of a normal speculative development with dwellings of conventional depth spaced along a typical access road. The steepness of the site confounded them, as such a layout would have required excessive cut-and-fill and steep driveways. In order to avoid major site works, retaining walls and stepped superstructures, a range of wide frontage, shallow depth houses of controlled aspect was developed. These were sited along contours on slopes of about 7° to 5° (1 in 8 to 1 in 11). Access to both front and rear gardens has been possible without excessive site works. These units comprise two-bedroom, three-person, two-storey houses with a common depth of only 3.9 m. The respective areas of 56.16 and 62.42 m^2 are some 15 per cent below Parker Morris sizes, and the dwellings are simply furnished and equipped. Great care however has been taken with the way the units can be grouped together, and much thought has been given to external materials and landscaping. The high proportion of small houses (none with more than four nominal bedspaces) gives a density of 130 bedspaces per hectare. Although this density is considerably higher than that in the initial sketch layout by the Local Authority, it is achieved without undue overcrowding.

Apart from the decision to adopt shallow depth controlled aspect dwellings, no other architectural device was used to overcome the slope. The strength of this scheme lies in the initial planning decision to develop a semi-Radburn layout

(a)

(b)

Fig. 3.28a, b Arden Estate, Banbury: wide frontage shallow depth houses have been built mostly along the contours.

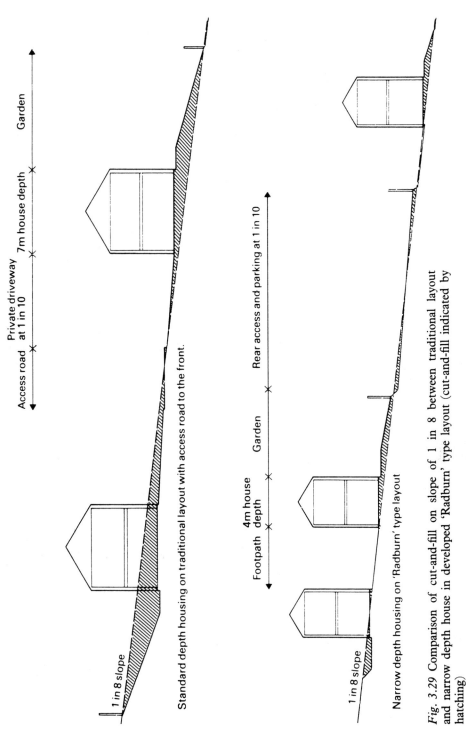

Fig. 3.29 Comparison of cut-and-fill on slope of 1 in 8 between traditional layout and narrow depth house in developed 'Radburn' type layout (cut-and-fill indicated by hatching)

57

along the existing contours. Such a plan produces a variety of public and private spaces without undue engineering problems.

The soil at Banbury is clay and presented no particular problems. However, traditional strip footings were employed rather than raft or trenchfill, so that any local discrepancies in site levels could be accommodated by adding or subtracting extra courses of facing brick to take up the immediate slopes.

The houses on this estate were designed to sell at 1981 prices of between £13,950 and £19,500, which represents good value. The scheme does not aim to break new ground in architectural form, but does show what can be done by other means with considerable environmental and financial advantages.

It is interesting to compare the selected scheme at Banbury with the three unsuccessful tenders. All four schemes aimed to provide dwellings of similar cost and two of the schemes not chosen would have had higher densities than the selected scheme. One of these, with a density 7 per cent greater than the Timms scheme, produced an interesting linear layout with roads and terraced housing built along the contours. It attempted the difficult but desirable goal of providing direct access to each house but the result would almost certainly have produced an unsightly array of garage frontages. From the site sections it also appears that the true steepness of some of the site had not been fully considered.

The scheme with the greatest number of units (156) made no comment in the accompanying report about the conditions of slope. The layout had a series of standard flat-site houses completely disregarding the gradients. In the last scheme, the developer also proposed his standard house type and in the report attention is given to the placing of the houses into identifiable groups with the road pattern influenced by the steep gradient across the site.

From the schemes proposed for the Banbury site it is clear that two of the four entrants had barely considered the implications of slope while a third proposed an idea which would have been workable only after more detailed design. At this scale of operation, where margins between success and failure are so small, wholly successful ideas are only possible if thoughtful effort is made at the design stage. This is borne out by the Timms/Charter Design scheme. The small difference between successful and unsuccessful schemes perhaps also explains why so few speculative developers are prepared to put more effort into design.

Cwmbran

A similar solution to the Banbury scheme has been arrived at by the Architects Department at Cwmbran New Town in Gwent where slopes of 11° or 12° (1 in 5) are quite common and a variety of design types have been adopted. At one stage, a courtyard plan was adopted with vehicular access and parking within the centre of the enclosed space. Such a form, however, was not sympathetic to the slope, creating awkward steps in the terraces, and as the sides of the courtyard are of varying levels, there is little sense of the enclosure and identity which the plan sought to create. It is interesting to see the development and improvement of this idea, with the courtyards gradually 'unwinding' until, at Thornhill IV, built in

Fig. 3.30 Courtyard plan can create awkward junctions and details. Cwmbran, Gwent.

1982, curving terraces follow the natural contours of the slopes between 10° and 5° (1 in 6 to 1 in 11).

For reasons of economy and ease of constructing both houses and engineering works, it is simpler wherever possible to build along the contours. Such a layout also has the advantage of achieving the most unobstructed views, especially if the site is relatively steep and the distances between the dwellings allow views over the houses downslope.

The shape and orientation of the site however, and the desire to avoid monotonous layout, may mean that some houses are positioned across or even at right angles to the contours. Where there is a steep north-facing (northern hemisphere) slope, the lack of sunlight may be alleviated by positioning houses facing east-west, with the service roads along the contours.

Density and the degree of vehicle penetration on to individual plots are also significant factors governing the choice of layout. The design selected for the Arden Estate at Banbury achieves much of its success through the negative virtue of not allowing the houses to have private parking within the curtilage. Many would claim that the accommodation of the private car within each plot is necessary. Layouts with terraces at right angles on slopes steeper than about 5° (1 in 10) or even those which create private driveways steeper than about 7° (1 in 8) will make this requirement difficult to achieve. The imposition of the motor vehicle and garaging is a greater problem on sloping sites than on the flat, and is only adequately resolved by the more radical forms and solutions described in later sections.

59

Sunlight and daylight

The need to permit adequate sunlighting and daylighting is clearly related to density since on north-facing slopes the possibility of overshadowing can cause the need to separate dwellings or rows of dwellings more widely than on the flat.

Department of the Environment standards for council housing indicate that the sides of housing facing south or any direction east or west of south should, on 1 March, have all points at least 2 m above ground level accessible for sunlight for at least 3 hours. Sunlight is counted only if the sun is at least 10° above the horizon but sunlight at a bearing of less than $22\frac{1}{2}°$ to the side of the building is not excluded. For buildings facing north or any direction east or west of north including due east, there should be a sky component of at least 0.84 per cent between bearings of 45° to the normal and elevations of 10° and 30° upwards at all points 2 m above ground level. (For further details see Department of the Environment 1971 and British Standards Institute 1945.)

Such standards and other desirable criteria such as sunlight on north-facing sides and north-facing gardens can be achieved by careful house design and layout. There are three main measures which can assist.

On north-facing slopes a long, sloping roof of no more than about 40° elevation (at the latitudes of the UK) can enable summer sun to reach most parts of north-facing gardens. Rooflights will allow a small amount of direct summer sunlight even on the north face. This principle has been employed at Frankley in Birmingham on a north-facing slope of about 14° (1 in 4).

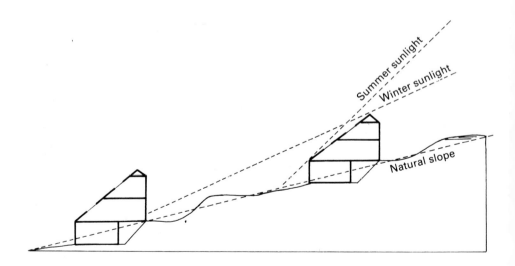

Fig. 3.31 Some direct sunlight is possible even on a steep north-facing slope as at Frankley, Birmingham

Fig. 3.32 Some summer sun penetrates through the rooflights of this Birmingham City Council housing at Frankley, despite being on a 14° (1 in 4) north-facing slope

Fig. 3.33 On a slope of 14° (1 in 4) it is hardly possible to avoid steep, awkward gardens . . .

Fig. 3.34 ... and a small patio has been provided next to each house. Privacy equals that on many flat sites. Frankley, Birmingham

A similar principle was employed at Basildon (Madge 1975) on a large estate of 556 dwellings on a more gentle north-facing slope. Basically, the dwellings comprise a single storey with kitchen area and access on the north and two-storey living and bedroom accommodation facing south. Both levels have easy access to the garden (Fig. 3.35).

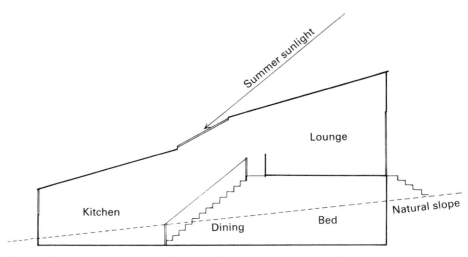

Fig. 3.35 A design for getting direct sunlight on a gentle, north-facing slope

Another device which can allow direct sunlight into north-facing rooms is the clerestory (Fig. 3.36). By the use of housing of reduced overall height and lower northern elevations than more conventional housing, such designs can similarly reduce the effects of the need for direct sunlight on overall housing density.

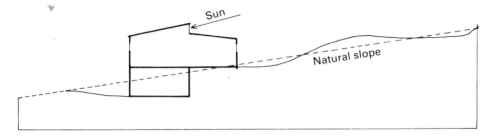

Fig. 3.36 The clerestory is a way of getting direct sunlight on a north-facing slope

In hot climates it may be desirable to arrange overhangs so that winter sun is allowed to enter but summer sun is not. Various other arrangements of this kind are explained in Scott and Furphy Engineers (1979).

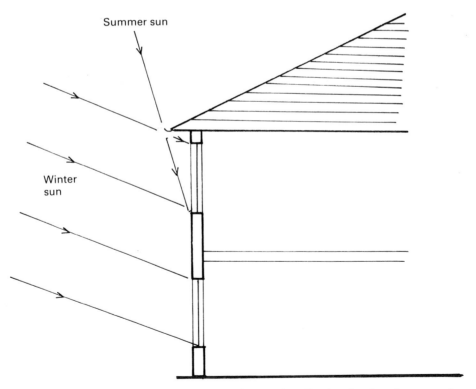

Fig. 3.37 Overhangs are a device in hot climates for allowing in the winter sun but keeping out the summer sun

63

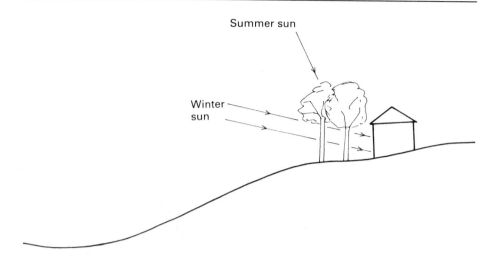

Fig. 3.38 Trees can also be useful in hot climates for keeping out the summer sun and allowing in the winter sun

A further problem of sunlighting and daylighting on slopes is that with a north-facing aspect; some of the sunlight available does not reach the main living rooms usually facing north and south if the houses are built with service roads along the contours. One solution, especially where there is also an eastwards or westwards element in the direction of slope, is to build facing east-west of short cul-de-sacs at right angles to the contours. For two-storey houses this may well add to road costs and reduce density significantly but for flats or maisonettes, which can be reached directly from service roads parallel to the contours, much of this problem may be avoided.

Privacy

Rooms and garden areas looking downslope have greater privacy than on the level because the points from which they can be seen are at a lower level. This may be a particular advantage where there is a footpath or road nearby downslope: the residents will be able to look out from normally positioned windows.

Any problems of privacy will be for rooms and garden areas looking upslope. A lot can be achieved with fencing and planting and by consideration of layouts, particularly footpaths in relation to the parts liable to be overlooked. Even when looking upslope, building across the slope can result in increased privacy (Fig. 3.42).

A sloping site therefore causes some aspects of a house to be more liable to be overlooked from public spaces outside and neighbouring properties. On the other hand, other aspects of the same house are likely to be more private than on a level site. Slopes therefore afford an opportunity for internal design and site layouts to

64

Fig. 3.39 The steep slopes of this restricted site in Kendal, Cumbria, have been terraced to create flat platforms for small two-storey houses. Note the asymmetrical roof form: by building the 'up slope' first floor rooms into the pitch, the bulk of the house is reduced, allowing more light to penetrate between the terraces. The slope is south facing

be drawn up bearing in mind differing requirements for privacy in different parts of the house.

Density

Often it is unclear when designing for slopes whether land areas have been measured from a flat plan or by site survey. The areas measured, and therefore density, will be considerably different on all but gentle gradients.

65

Fig. 3.40 Overlooking is usually a problem on sloping sites, but can be reduced with careful site planning. Blackburn, Lancashire

Fig. 3.41 Narrow upstairs windows help to maintain privacy in this housing by Birmingham City Council at Frankley

Fig. 3.42 A slope can help to increase rather than reduce
privacy if used properly

Unless retaining walls are used, which can be both expensive and unsightly,
the need to grade land within a dwelling curtilage may reduce density
considerably. Where the slope is at right angles to the house frontage for example
a 10 m frontage on a slope of 5.4° (1 in 10) will result in a 1 m difference between
ends. If this is graded at 26° (1 in 2) then an extra 2 m would be needed, making
a 12 m frontage. Slopes at right angles to the frontage incur the worst possible
problems in this respect. In other cases, some allowance for regrading can be made
in the front or back garden. This way of regrading is most common in countries
where densities are otherwise relatively low. It is not common in the UK.

Retaining walls are an alternative to regrading. In purely economic terms, if it
is assumed that regrading would be at a gradient of 26 ° (1 in 2) then a retaining

wall will save an area of land twice its size. The cost of wall and land may thus be compared. There may however be variations in the market value of otherwise similar housing using the two solutions as a result of differences in appearance and the amount of open garden around the houses.

In the northern hemisphere on a north-facing slope the need for sunlight and its effects on the desirable distances between dwellings will be another factor to consider which may limit density to below that which would be acceptable in terms of other criteria such as privacy.

At high latitudes in the northern hemisphere, daylight and sunlight standards may result in the distance between dwellings (or rows of dwellings) being greater than they would need to be to meet other criteria such as distance for privacy and the need for gardens and other open space around buildings. The Joint Housing Development Unit of the Scottish Development Department has developed a computer program to take into account constraints including sunlight, daylight and privacy standards, road lengths, open space need and gradients for roads and footpaths. From an input of values for the constraints and data on house type and mix, layout pattern, slope and orientation, the program generates optimum density, cost per person for external works, site development and substructure (Scottish Development Department 1972). The program has four main uses:

1. To explore the relationship between the five variables of shell size, house mix, site slope, layout and orientation. How does density vary with slope? Does density on a given slope vary with house type or with layout pattern?

2. Two special house types have been developed. The first is a split level house with its living room half a floor above the entrance, allowing blocks to be placed closer together whilst maintaining sunlight standards. The second is a standard shell but one side has no daylighting or sunlighting windows. The blocks can therefore be placed close together running down the sloped to form narrow pedestrian ways.

3. To measure the effects of relaxing constraints, particularly daylighting and sunlighting standards.

4. The program has been used to abstract substructure packages and to generate bills of quantities.

Density is therefore affected by both the orientation of dwellings in relation to the slope and by the compass orientation of the slope, but particularly by the latter. The costs of roads and public utility services outside the dwelling curtilage will also be affected by both but it is difficult to say whether one is likely to be more significant than the other. The length of roads and other services per dwelling will tend to increase with decreasing density, or in an attempt to fit orientation of dwellings to slope.

Sometimes a sloping site is an advantage in achieving higher density than on the flat, especially if it is south-facing. On gradients steeper than about 9° (1 in 6) one possible house form comprises an extra storey on the downslope side (as explained in the next chapter). This extra storey often includes the garage which, in effect, has been accommodated without taking up any extra land area. As a more general principle, building into a slope results in more floor area for a given site. On very steep slopes, cascade dwellings are a common solution (see next chapter) in which several or all floors have direct access to ground level. The schemes at Cefn-coed-y-cymmer, St Ann's (Nottingham) and Oakenshaw 5 (Redditch) explained in the next chapter all illustrate this principle. Such schemes can achieve very high densities.

Stepped section housing at Queensmere Road, Wimbledon (London) (Plumb 1976) overcame a slope of more than 7° (1 in 8) using a solution similar in principle to those just mentioned but rather less extreme in design. Ground conditions prevented building above four storeys. The slope faces south with roads running east–west. Upslope, on the northern side of the road, garages and pedestrian access are at road level with a maisonette and flat above. On the downslope side of the road, access is again at road level leading to one maisonette above road level and one below. Stepping has reduced the visual impact of these dwellings. The density is 284 persons per hectare.

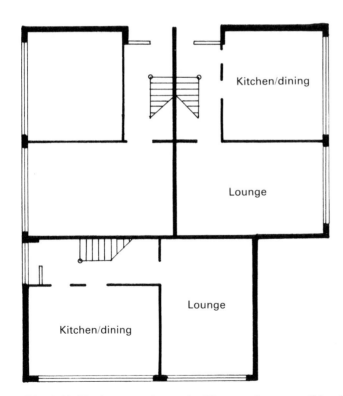

Fig. 3.43 Single aspect cluster dwellings can be compatible with increased densities

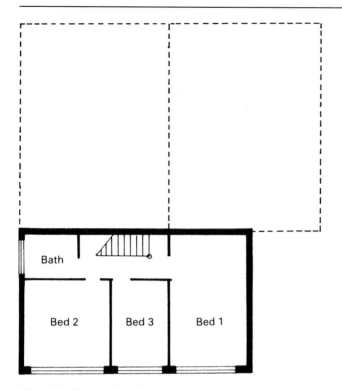

Fig. 3.44 Upper floor plan

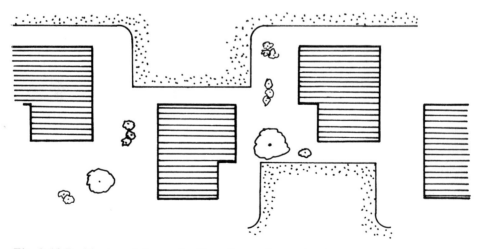

Fig. 3.45 Positioning of cluster dwellings for maximum density

On another part of the same site at Wimbledon where the gradient is 7° (1 in 8) a density of 202 persons per hectare has been achieved with five- and six-person, two-storey single aspect dwellings built in clusters of three (Fig. 3.43 to 3.45). A similar cluster is positioned 21.3 m away to achieve privacy. A third cluster is positioned between but staggered.

At Addington near Croydon (London) a section of the Forestdale development had been developed by Wates Ltd down a south-facing hillside. A series of eleven single storey flat-roof blocks cascade down the hillside, giving a total of sixty one- and two-bedroom dwellings each with a south-facing patio off the dining room. Despite a density of thirty-seven dwellings per acre, the standard of privacy is reported to be good (*Building*, 16 April 1971 pp 90–91).

Garaging

Achieving driveways of gradient so as to avoid scraping the exhaust is a potential problem on slopes steeper than about 5° or 6° (1 in10). Steep driveways are also more difficult to use by drivers and are a safety hazard, particularly in winter due to ice and snow. The problem in the UK arises out of the desire for garaging within the house curtilage for easy access and to reduce vandalism and the desire for single family houses (rather than flats). In Stockholm, for example, the problem of garaging on slopes seems much less despite having a much greater frequency of

Fig. 3.46 Almost a flat site design with use of downslope for garaging. Dividing the garage courts certainly makes them less obtrusive. High density, unobtrusiveness of the car and careful attention to natural landscaping are some of the hallmarks of some of Stockholm's mass housing. Hässelby, near Stockholm, Sweden

Fig. 3.47 Unobtrusive garaging at Hässelby near Stockholm, Sweden

sloping sites than most British cities. The greater acceptance of flats with grouped garages and the highly subsidized and frequent public transport system (which makes frequent use and ownership of private cars less essential in some districts than in British cities) contribute to this difference.

One solution is to group garages in courts on flatter parts of the site. This however is not usually a popular solution with residents, partly due to inconvenience, or to the risk of vandalism in these courts. Most planning authorities would not allow garaging in front of the building line due to its visual effects, but in any case, this would not often give much scope for avoiding or easily modifying the slope.

Where land is sloping steeply upwards from the road access, cutting into the earth is quite a straightforward solution. Garages built at least partly into the earth are quite common and present no special construction problems. There are a number of such examples in the next chapter at St Ann's, Nottingham, Redditch and Frankley.

Garaging where the land from the road access slopes steeply downwards is more of a problem. Some cut-and-fill can be a solution on slopes of up to about 8° (1 in 7). Otherwise the garage or parking space may be raised entirely above ground, though with extra cost of car-bearing construction and with the disadvantage of making the car parking space visually very prominent (see Figs. 4.17 and 4.18).

On very steep slopes where forms of cascade dwellings are employed, car parking is often possible by any of various forms of internal circulation within the building (see for example St Ann's, Nottingham, and Cefn-coed-y-cymmer in the next chapter and the Oslo New Town of Holmlia, Oslo Kommune 1980; Neylan 1966).

Fig. 3.48 The parked car intrudes into the classical layout of Bath

Fig. 3.49 In housing areas laid out on slopes before the invention of the motor car, parked vehicles appear even more obtrusive than in layouts on flat sites. This is a problem both in 'organic' hill towns such as Bridgnorth or classical ones such as Bath. Careful design in recent housing schemes can take advantage of the slope to conceal vehicles

Fig. 3.50 Where the extra storey downslope is used for garaging, care is needed to avoid a desolate, barracks-like appearance . . . Blackburn, Lancashire

Fig. 3.51 Garages at Cwmbran built at half-level below 'ground' floor

Fig. 3.52 This garage is tucked neatly away upslope. Perhaps the slope itself draws attention away from the garage to the opposite side of the house. Shelf near Bradford

Fig. 3.53 Garage courts need particularly sensitive planning on slopes to avoid a gaping, open view of the inside of the court and main vistas from downslope. Banbury

Fig. 3.54 On the other hand, land slope can be used to reduce the visual effects of a garage court. Enclosing the entrance near to the flank walls of main residential buildings also helps to reduce the visual effect. This is very much more an inward looking layout than that at Banbury. Harborne, Birmingham

Fig. 3.55 Another way of hiding garaging is inside a courtyard. However this may create a nuisance to residents in the form of noise and fumes, and will certainly raise the cost of building the houses. Some may also wonder how far one visual problem has been replaced by another. Banbury, Oxfordshire

Fig. 3.56 Although no less prominent, a pitched roof perhaps makes the garage less ugly. As well as raising the question of safety, using the footpath as a driveway also makes this look even more like a 'garage with house'. Blackburn, Lancashire

Steep driveways are also a safety hazard. Post *et al.* (1978) have studied the hazard caused by steep drives and the costs of building to lesser gradients. They conclude that the most cost-effective gradient is 7° (1 in 8), in terms of achievement compared to the cost of road safety measures.

Roads and other services on slopes

The slopes of roads and other infrastructure are not necessarily the same as those of the site. Indeed, layouts are often designed so that roads are parallel or diagonal to the contours and consequently of a lesser gradient, particularly on steep slopes of more than about 5° (1 in 11) where the gradient starts to become a serious constraint for both construction and usage. In the USA, for example, many road codes forbid construction of streets steeper than 5.4° to 4.5° (1 in 10 to 1 in 12) (House Builders, National Association of, USA 1974).

On any slope, a greater length of any infrastructure service will be needed compared to a flat land surface of the same area in plan. Also there are additional costs for trenching which are particularly serious for slopes greater than about 7° (1 in 8) where some forms of mechanical equipment cannot be used.

Roads and pathways on sloping sites raise at least three issues.

1. Their location plays a big part in determining the views and sequence of vistas from public space on the site. The upper reaches will give the longest and perhaps the best view if uninterrupted by building in the foreground, though

sometimes at the expense of bleakness and exposure. This may be alleviated by the planting of trees and bushes as windbreaks or by careful consideration of the building layouts in relation to the prevailing wind. On the lower slopes, enclosure may be the aim.

2. The convenience and safety of using roads and pathways, particularly when there is ice and snow.

3. Construction costs, which along with those of most public utility services, tend to be higher on sloping sites.

On steep slopes, the construction of all services raises problems for the use of mechanical equipment. These problems vary greatly according to the nature of the equipment to be used, but it would be quite common for a slope of 5° (1 in 11) to create difficulties for some methods of road laying and very likely that a slope of 9° (1 in 6) would inhibit the use of many forms of mechanical equipment.

It is not possible to relate the costs to slope accurately except in particular case studies. Nor is it possible to produce accurate generalizations because costs are also affected by the following:

(a) Variability of angle of slope. It has been shown in Sweden (Svenska Byggnadsentreprenoerfoeriningen 1976) that one combined change in gradient and level are cheaper than two changes in gradient. Variability of slope will also affect the amount and cost of cut-and-fill.

Fig. 3.57 Car parking spaces raised above surrounding footpaths are emphasized. Blackburn, Lancashire

(a)

(b)

Fig. 3.58a, b In order to avoid a steep gradient to the garages upslope, the road has been planned at a high level. In anything other than a quiet cul-de-sac such as this, traffic would be a nuisance to the houses downslope. Blackburn, Lancashire

Fig. 3.59 At Darwen, the gradients of parking spaces have been kept reasonable despite the steepness of the site. Also, the definition of land use is clear and unambiguous

Fig. 3.60 A block of flats is wrapped around a very steep rocky hillside at Färsta near Stockholm. Even on very steep sites quite modest cutting and the placing of roads diagonal to the contours can achieve fairly gentle gradients. The footpath down to the suburban railway station takes a more direct route using steps

Fig. 3.61 Note the ribbed pavement, giving grip to pedestrians in this steeply sloping street in Bridgnorth

Fig. 3.62 Terraced housing of 'amended section' face across the river Avon to the centre of historic Bath

Fig. 3.63 Main footpaths run along the contour between these terraced houses overlooking Bath. The houses on the left are of three storeys: living rooms are on the top floor, to take advantage of the view over the lower terraces; vehicular access (to integral garage) from the rear on the middle level; bedrooms are on this level and on the garden level below

(b) The amount of excavations and kind of bedrock which depend on variability of slope and standards to be adopted.

A number of computer programs are available from the Transport and Road Research Laboratory, Crowthorne, Berkshire RG11 6AU, which can predict road construction costs and vehicle operating costs according to various physical conditions including land slope.

However, a rough indication of the order of costs involved for road construction on slopes for use in initial estimating may be derived from graph 1 of Gee (1962):

Road costs per unit length as % on flat land	1:25	1:20	1:15	1:10	1:9	1:8	1:7	1:6	1:5
	103	104	106	108	109	112	116	125	147

These figures refer to cost per unit length. It is also important to remember that the length of road on slopes is also greater than on the level.

Of the other services, it is sewerage which usually presents the most problems on steep slopes. Careful design is needed to maintain service connections at a standard depth. Very flat land on the other hand can cause problems of achieving a gradient in services at a reasonable depth. It may be necessary to construct artificial high and low points with earthworks.

Fig. 3.64 Stepped footpath runs up the slope between these 'amended section' terraces in Bath. The facing materials are a rather unhappy attempt to be 'in keeping' with the classical, stone-faced housing of historic Bath.

It has been quite common for deep digs to result from poor layout and from the belief that steep gradients on sewers and high velocities result in excessive scour. However, Department of the Environment Working Party on Sewers and Water Mains (Department of the Environment 1968) has shown that scour in pipes is much more closely related to the amount of abrasive material than the velocity. In fact, the depth of erosion along the line of invert is reduced with increasing velocity up to 7.6 m per second, the erosion being spread over a wider arc. These findings relate to straight pipes. At bends and other irregularities erosion did increase with velocity. Previous practice of restricting gradients increased construction costs. The Working Party estimates that 7.5 per cent in drainage costs could be saved even in Ipswich, a comparatively flat town where the party's main study was carried out. It should also be remembered that increasing the velocity of drainage on a gradient will tend to reduce the size of pipes necessary together with their cost.

Particularly where the gradient is variable, there may be a large number of changes in direction of sewerage mains and therefore the need for a large number of manholes. This is an important element in costing. Pumping is also costly and its necessity should be incorporated into the early stages of site planning.

Fig. 3.65 Manholes are an important extra cost resulting from changes in direction of sewerage mains, both horizontal and vertical

In general, therefore, a slight gradient of perhaps 1° or 2° (1 in 25 to 1 in 30) is ideal for drainage purposes. Steeper than this, it becomes increasingly likely that drop manholes will be necessary to limit the gradient of the pipe while maintaining sewers at a workable depth. These add greatly to cost, for they can easily double the costs per unit length. Extra lengths will also be needed. On the other hand, at steeper gradients, increased velocity will mean that more houses can be served from a pipe of given diameter.

For water supply, maintenance of a head of water is an additional problem on some sloping sites, though it is at least as much affected by the general height of the area to be served as by gradient.

Gas, electricity supply and telecommunications are rarely seriously affected by gradient. Although high voltage electricity cables filled with oil can, on long slopes, result in problems from the build-up of oil pressure. Also, there may be extra costs for sub-stations if these too have to be built on a steep gradient. Generally however the costs effects of slope are very small per house served.

Chapter 4

House design

Choice of design adaptation

In the previous chapter, three basic reactions to sloping sites were identified – by layout, landform manipulation and by special house designs. Layouts were the main concern of that chapter. Here we go on to examine the two other approaches to dealing with slope.

Six methods of adapting and designing houses to accommodate slope can be identified:

1. *Extra masonry.* Minor amendments can be made to construction such as increasing the number of courses of masonry on the downward side of the slope. From this adapted plinth, standard flat site dwellings can then be constructed.

2. *Cut-and-fill.* The site can be modelled to produce flat areas on which to construct houses otherwise designed for flat sites. This method is the building response to the 'landform adapted' approach to layout identified earlier.

3. *Amended section.* The plan and section of an otherwise normal house can be amended so that certain areas occupy different levels. In elongated forms such as bungalows, rooms at the end of the plan can be placed up or down a few steps: with more compact designs, areas such as garages and entrance halls may be placed a whole storey above or, more often, below an otherwise standard unit.

4. *Split level.* Special split level designs, usually with a series of floors half a storey height apart, can be used. In these solutions, the implications of the sloping site are apparent right through the plan, section and construction of the whole dwelling.

5. *Cascade.* For schemes on steeper slopes, and often for those developed at high densities, a cross-section in the form of a pulled-out chest of drawers can be employed, with the staggered floors stepping down the contours. Such forms can be either subdivided horizontally into flats or maisonettes, or vertically into terraced housing.

6. *Houses on posts*. The dwelling can be built off a platform, at or above the highest level where the 'ground' floor comes into contact with the natural ground form. The building then stands on a horizontal deck with the land virtually untouched, falling beneath it.

These variations are shown in diagrammatic form in Fig. 4.1. It will be appreciated that there is an overlap between the approaches to layout identified earlier and the design of individual units. This requires close collaboration between those who identify sites for housing and those who produce the initial layouts and the more detailed designs. Early understanding of the problems and possibilities of sloping sites should prevent awkward and uneconomic solutions and help produce creative and cost-effective schemes.

Simple adaptation of the structure – extra courses of masonry

A very common solution on shallow slopes in simply to add extra courses of bricks on the downward side. A extra course of bricks might result in additional costs of £40 to £70 depending on the perimeter affected, which would result in extra costs of perhaps £150 to £300 per dwelling on a slope of 3° (1 in 19) (first quarter 1983 prices).

There are many examples of this simple adaptation, a typical one being at Manor Hill, Tamworth, where a section of a private sector estate of 279 houses was built on a natural ground slope of 4.5° (1 in 12) at an angle of 20° to it. The houses are all two-storey semi-detached of 70 m² floor area. Ground slope was accommodated by extra courses of bricks averaging ten per dwelling at an extra cost of £450 per dwelling (second quarter 1981 price) or 3 per cent of construction costs excluding land acquisition. To accommodate cut on an adjacent part of the site, a retaining wall 55 m in length by 6 m in height was also necessary at a cost of £10,000.

Adaptation of the site; cut-and-fill

Again, this is a very common solution, often used as the only measure on gentle slopes of approximately 5° (1 in 11) or less, or in combination with other adaptations on steeper slopes. The cut material usually occupies a greater volume than when in its natural state, though after compaction, this may be up to 10 per cent less. The amount of compaction, can, within limits, be a matter of choice, the ideal being to aim for a soil which is sufficiently compacted to avoid settlement after building, but not so compacted that the soil structure is destroyed so that drainage is impeded.

Overturning of the topsoil will destroy its profile to some extent, even if conservation measures are taken. This will encourage erosion even on very gentle slopes with loss of soil and silting with pollution downstream. This can be greatly reduced by staging the earthworks with quick seeding and replanting or by construction of low earth dams on the downstream side of the construction site.

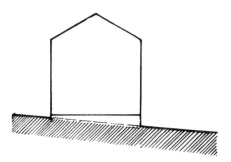

Fig. 4.1a Extra masonry – plinth built up to form a level platform for normal flat site dwelling

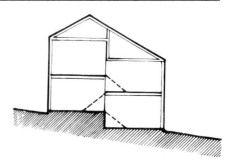

Fig. 4.1b Split level – special plan and section: usually based on half storey change of level

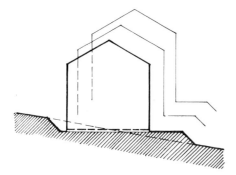

Fig. 4.1c Cut-and-fill – site modelled to create level plots; steps and staggers sometimes employed to maintain ground floor of each house close to natural level

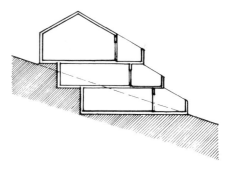

Fig. 4.1d Cascade – staggered cross section: off-sets depend on gradient. These can be sub-divided horizontally or vertically into individual dwellings

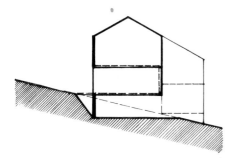

Fig. 4.1e Amended section – floors within each dwelling at different levels to suit site; garage sometimes forms lowest storey beneath otherwise standard dwelling or, depending on position of roads, is placed at upper level

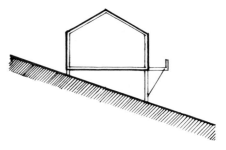

Fig. 4.1f Houses on posts – dwellings built on platform completely divorced from ground

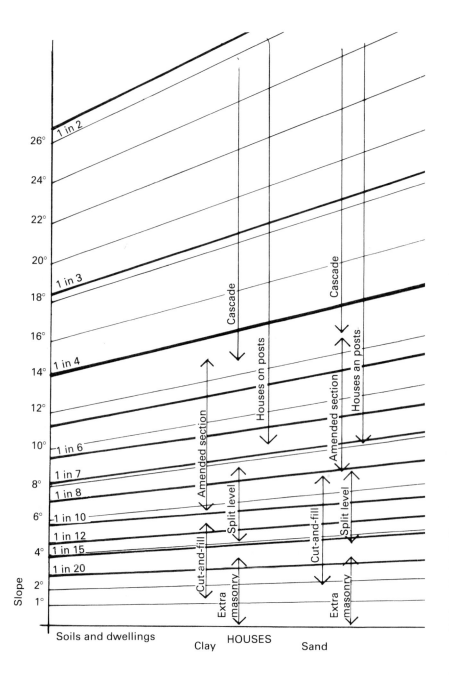

Fig. 4.2

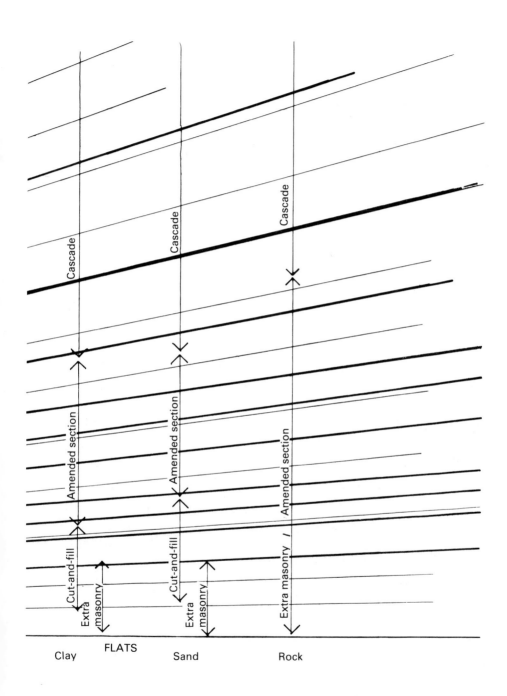

Cascade

Cascade

Cascade

Amended section

Amended section

Amended section

Cut-and-fill

Cut-and-fill

Extra masonry

Extra masonry

Extra masonry

Clay FLATS Sand Rock

Fig. 4.3 Manor Hill, Tamworth – private sector estate on a slope of about 4.5° (1 in 12)

Fig. 4.4 The extra masonry beneath these houses in Kingstanding, Birmingham, is clearly identified by a different coloured brick. This row, and the housing on Fig. 3.6, are within 182 m (200 yards), showing different approaches to slope in the same locality

Fig. 4.5 A typical example of extra courses of masonry on the 'downslope' beneath an otherwise standard flat site design. Note that the complications of even shallow slopes extend to influence external works. (House on private estate, Oakham, Leics)

Attention must also be given to the steepness of the new slopes created by cut-and-fill which over small sections can often be greater than the original. The maximum slope desirable depends greatly on plant cover and subsoil as explained in Chapter 5.

Three problems are often associated with cut-and-fill:

1. There can be a need for extra damp proofing on the wall of the house facing up slope. Often, non-habitable rooms such as the garage are placed in this

91

position. In semi-detached housing, this will usually result in some garages having external side-walls facing downslope perhaps built off retaining walls. In such circumstances it is important to ensure adequate depth of foundation on the garage end-wall as well as the side-walls. Shrinkage, particularly on clay soils, is liable to cause cracking in external garage end-walls (Bickerdyke, Allen and Bramble 1974).

2. There are usually problems of compaction of the fill, particularly on soils with a high clay content. Although for light structures it may be safe to found part of the building on fill provided it is properly compacted and the formation underlying the fill properly prepared (Abbott and Pollit 1980 p 255), for heavier buildings the foundations should normally go below the fill to avoid differential settlement.

3. A problem associated with cut-and-fill is that, depending on substrata, angle of slope and plant available, cut-and-fill may be economically viable only over quite small sites. Even the site of a pair of semi-detached houses may be too big, cut-and-fill being carried out separately for each house. In this case, and more commonly where a terrace runs across the contours, the houses have to be stepped, with extra external walls and flashings in between.

Work carried out by Patrick Todd of Wimpey Construction UK Ltd. gives an interesting comparison between simple adaptation with extra masonry and adapting the site by cut-and-fill. Extra costs above those on level ground were calculated for a standard semi-detached house of 5.22 m width and 7.51 m depth (area 78 m^2) with a slope from back to front of 9° (1 in 6).

In the first case, it was assumed that there would be no regrade, no driveway or garage space, because (as the slope would be too steep without regrade). Also, there would be a suspended slab on approved fill and that the plot would be developed in isolation. Construction costs for extra items above normal construction (at July 1981 prices) were calculated to be as follows:

	(£)
Brickwork	174.59
Load-bearing wall	220.90
Concrete to foundation	10.63
Concrete to suspended floor slab	101.85
Steps	7.00
Handrail	3.11
Excavations to foundations	7.25
Reinforcement	113.68
	639.01

In the second (cut-and-fill) case it was assumed that there would be regrade to front, back and driveway to reduce the slope of 9° to 1.6° (1 in 6 to 1 in 29) and that there would be a driveway 3 m wide to the side of each house. A level for regrade was chosen 600 mm above existing ground level at the lower end of the slab. This eliminated the need for a suspended slab and allowed for a ground level 150 mm above a step in the foundation. Costs for extra items above normal construction (at July 1981 prices) were calculated to be as follows:

	(£)
Cut for floor slab	40.00
Fill for floor slab	56.70
Brickwork	24.75
Excavation to foundation	0.77
Concrete to foundation (2 steps)	4.24
Cut to drive	28.62
Fill to drive	30.46
Cut to rear garden	262.20
Fill to front garden	52.60
Carting away material	515.65
	1,015.22

Although more expensive on the assumptions made, the regrading solution included works to driveways and gardens not included in the first case. Excluding these, the costs would have been £639.01 (no regrade) compared with £641.34 (regrade). The cases also show the sensitivity of regrade solutions to carting costs. In a site which is part of a large estate, they may well be lower than the figure assumed and in fact the regrade solution could be cheaper overall.

A third alternative would be to regrade rather less: to 5.4° (1 in 10) for driveways with no regrade for front and rear gardens. This would necessitate a small wall at the front and a retaining wall at the rear. Even assuming a drive of only 2.45 m width, however, such a scheme would be considerably more expensive, largely due to the retaining wall:

	(£)
Cut for floor slab	90.29
Fill to underside of slab	8.04
Brickwork	161.80
Excavation to foundations	11.23
Steps	14.00
Handrail	10.08
Perforated land drain	143.00
Concrete to foundations	7.09
Cut to drive	77.09
Retaining wall	760.00
Carting away material	437.21
	1,719.83

The relative viability of these schemes will be greatly affected by works to neighbouring plots, all these studies assuming that development takes place in

93

isolation. The provisions for dumping excess cut material will also be very significant.

Remodelling the contours to achieve flat terraced areas for standard house types and to create acceptable gradients for access roads and driveways is a method favoured by many private sector developers and some local authorities, especially those who do not have large design offices to produce more specialized purpose-built solutions.

Burnley

In Burnley, a small (131 dwelling) development built in the late 1970s was cut-and-filled to allow the borough to place standard flat site designs: all the necessary alterations to design occurred below the ground floor slab. The particular unit chosen for comparison was a four-bedroom, five-person house of approximately 97 m^2 with a plan shape of 7.5 m by 5.5 m and a 3.0 m by 2.5 m bay on two floors. This comprised 29 per cent of the total development. Construction is of load-bearing masonry with timber roofs built off strip foundations. The original gradients varied up to 8° (1 in 7). The final layout consists of short, two-storey terraces. No terrace is longer than ten units, the majority being four to six and some as little as three. The design density is 120 bedspaces per hectare.

Seven terraces have been chosen for cost analysis, one straight block built on flat ground and another straight block built almost entirely on fill. The other five terraces have steps between some dwellings on the line of the party wall, or in some cases, steps and staggers on plan to keep the ground floor slabs of each unit as close as possible to the natural ground level.

Fig. 4.6 Stepping and staggering diagonally to the contours in Council Housing at Burnley

Fig. 4.7 Burnley: cut-and-fill, even on quite gentle slopes, often results in fairly flat platforms separated by sharp breaks of slope. Some sense of enclosure, does, however, seem to have been created on this fairly gentle slope

Fig. 4.8 Burnley: flat site designs with cut-and-fill, retaining walls and breaks in roof line on a fairly gentle slope

The costs of units in each of these seven terraces is noted in Table 4.1. Perhaps the most interesting fact to emerge from this study is that the cost of stepped and staggered units is almost identical, irrespective of the amount of stepping or staggering or the proportion of cut to fill beneath each block. In fact the steps vary between 250 mm and 1,200 mm and the staggers from 2 m to 3.5 m.

Taking the unit cost of the straight flat terrace on natural ground level as 100, the stepped and staggered dwellings have a factor of about 107. The most

Table 4.1 Cost analysis for site in Burnley

Type	Cut/fill	Original gradient to line of terrace	Basic superstr. (£)	Extra for steps or staggers (£)	Substruct (£)	Total (£)	Index	Substruct. as % superstruct.
No step, no stagger	none		7,918	0	980	8,890	100	12.37
6 units; 2 steps 1 stagger	75% fill	1:18 0°	7,918	375	1,187	9,480	106.6	14.99
6 units; 1 step no stagger	95% fill	1:7.5 45°	7,918	200	1,393	9,511	106.9	17.59
5 units; 2 steps 2 staggers	75% fill	1:15 30°	7,918	500	1,112	9,530	107.2	14.34
4 units; 1 step no stagger	95% fill	1:15 10°	7,918	250	1,374	9,542	107.3	17.32
4 units; 1 step no stagger	cut	1:12 10°	7,918	250	1,380	9,548	107.4	17.32
4 units; no step no stagger	fill	1:7.5 90°	7,918	0	2,121	10,039	112.9	27.54

expensive solution in this particular development is the straight flat-slabbed terrace constructed on fill. The original ground beneath this terrace had a cross-fall of about 7.5° (1 in 7.5) and resulted in a cost index of 112.9.

Comparing simply the relative proportions of substructure and superstructure costs, that for the flat site is 12.4 per cent, those for the stepped and staggered designs about 17 per cent with and nearly 27 per cent for the filled site.

From this particular example it appears that excessive manipulation of the ground to achieve a flat straight slab is not necessarily the most economical solution to mass housing on sloping sites.

Redditch (Oakenshaw 6)

The index of +7 per cent for stepping and staggering units appears however to tally with a more recent scheme in Redditch by the Development Corporation whose Architect's Department has produced a wide variety of solutions to the undulating topography of the town. Slopes on this particular north-east facing site of 2 ha average between 7° and 8° (1 in 8 and 1 in 7) and the project was developed at the relatively high density of 152 bedspaces per hectare in short terraces on either side of a spine access road. Of the twenty six terraces, only one has no step or stagger within it, and four others no stagger. Most contain both steps and staggers at each party wall, so that the layout appears to flow diagonally down the slope. An *ad hoc* of 7 per cent above the Housing Cost Yardstick was claimed for work to the foundations, gable walls and external works. The external works element of this well landscaped scheme amounted to 11 per cent of admissible dwelling costs and the site development works to 20 per cent of the total contract.

Fig. 4.9 Redditch Oakenshaw 6. Short terraces stagger diagonally down the slope. The landscaping has been carefully carried out both for an attractive appearance and to reduce soil erosion

Fig. 4.10 Walmley (Sutton Coldfield), large, wide-fronted houses almost at right angles to the slope on a long, narrow part of the site where it would be hard to achieve any other layout. No adaptation of building design at least above ground level

Fig. 4.11 Viewed from downslope, the roof lines of this private sector estate at Walmley have a rather angular appearance. The long, narrow shape of this part of the site and the market for larger detached houses possibly influenced the choice of house type and orientation which pays little attention to the slope

Sutton Coldfield

At Walmley (Sutton Coldfield) a section of a private sector estate has been built (1981) on a slope of 8° (1 in 7) with the frontages at 80° to the contours. The houses are two-storey detached with frontages of 11 m by 8 m depth and a floor area of 130 m^2. Ground slope was accommodated mainly by cut-and-fill, though also with some extra courses of bricks. Total extra costs due to slope amounted to 14 per cent of construction costs (excluding land acquisition and professional fees), these being made up as follows:

	Per cent
Foundation (raft) in addition to foundation costs on level ground	7.0
Retaining walls	5.4
Earthworks	1.6

The subsoil is Keuper Marl.

Brunei

Sometimes cut-and-fill can take on a very different and more radical form than that referred to so far, which has been written with the UK in mind. Ibrahim Yassin, Deputy Planning Commissioner of Brunei, while working at Aston University in 1980–81, examined solutions to building housing on sloping land in Brunei for comparison with the UK. In the Champaka Estate for example, which is about 2.5 km from the centre of the capital, Bandar Seri Begawan, three platforms were made on land naturally sloping as steep as 25° (1 in 2) in parts.

Excavations were made to cut down from 58 m (190 ft) above sea level to 39–42 m (129–138 ft) in the north-eastern part of the site and from 44 m to 28–39 m (145 ft to 93–128 ft) in the south with fill in the north-west of the site. The cost of the earthwork was $144.72 (£29.59) per square metre floor area (1976) which was between 33 per cent and 56 per cent of building costs (excluding servicing and land acquisition).

Major earthworks could have been avoided if lower density had been accepted. It is estimated that a reduction from 178 houses to 78 houses could have resulted in earthworks costs per house being reduced by about 33 per cent. The layout adopted also resulted in extra length of road per dwelling (10 m per dwelling) though in other schemes examined it was up to three times as much.

Sometimes cut-and-fill can take the form of flattening a hill or ridge top rather than cutting into a hillside. In the Taman Tasek Estate about 13 km from Bandar Seri Begawan, two hilltops with initial slopes averaging 14° to 7° (1 in 4 to 1 in 8) were levelled, using the cut material to form a series of terraces on the hillsides. Excavation costs were only $9.7/m^2 of housing (1977) or 4–5 per cent of building costs excluding servicing and land acquisition. Yassin estimated that the costs of land preparation by cut-and-fill were, however, about 30 per cent more than the costs of adapting the building to accommodate the slope.

Amended sections

On steeper gradients, where terracing to provide enough total area on which to place conventional housing is not practical, it is common to vary the levels of parts of the dwellings, sometimes by as much as a whole storey. A typical example is to use the ground floor downslope as a garage, entrance, utility room or perhaps some living accommodation such as the kitchen and possibly even bedrooms. Other storeys are built above this level, often extending further on the upslope side. Advantage is then taken of this elevation to achieve good prospect from the main living rooms. In the UK there is a tendency to place only 'service' rooms within the slope to avoid any possibility of moisture penetration into main living rooms.

Fig. 4.12 An extra storey downslope and an unbroken inclined ridge line accommodate slope across and parallel to the terrace. Haslingden, Lancashire

Some variations of this general method will contain less than a full storey height between the changes of floor level; this is especially common with elongated platforms and 'one-off' private houses built on commanding sites. More compact plans adopt a full change of storey height. Some may simply be conventional two-storey housing built over a garage and entrance area.

Bovis Homes are one of the few large private sector developers in the United Kingdom who use special designs to overcome slopes. Much of their work is in the West Country, where gradients are quite severe and where there is a market for houses with good (and often seaward) views. Bovis maintain that fully split level solutions, as described in the next section, are not economical to construct where the plan area is restricted, but they have developed a whole range of house types with floors on various levels, from a change of only three or four steps to whole storey heights.

Their preference is for a 'bridge' solution, which overcomes the problem of major earth retention and special construction by cutting the dwelling into a naturally retained bank and linking it with the ground by a bridge at the upper level. The entrance floor is sometimes used for the garage and usually for the

Fig. 4.13 Garages built on downslope, some beneath lowest floor of terrace housing (Hawksley, Birmingham)

Fig. 4.14 In some houses, the extra storey downslope is used for living accommodation facing south . . .

Fig. 4.15 ... and the garage is upslope. Woodgate Valley, Birmingham

Fig. 4.16 There are two ground floors in this house at Shelf, near Bradford

main living rooms providing a good prospect. The solution can be unpopular, however, with the local planning authority as the bridge structure can appear dominant.

If some earth retention against the upslope wall is accepted as on a small estate of private sector house at Ulverston, Cumbria, the intrusion of the bridge structure can be overcome. These houses have fine views from the upper level reception rooms across a sloping site of up to 11° (1 in 5) to Morecambe Bay and the Fells of North Yorkshire.

On a steeply sloping site near Newton Abbot in Devon, all the house types had to be specially adapted by the Bovis Design Team, with rooms at different levels and garages incorporated into the dwellings at the most convenient access point.

Fig. 4.17 Cut-and-fill usually results in some sections, often gardens, being made even steeper. Here at Harborne, Birmingham, this increased steepness has been used to create first floor level parking and access, though it creates almost basement conditions for part of the house and, arguably, is not visually attractive

Fig. 4.18 The 'bridge' solution; Harborne, Birmingham

103

Fig. 4.19 An older version of the 'bridge' principle. Use is made of differences in level to get separate access to flats. Harborne, Birmingham

Fig. 4.20 Use is made of differences in level to get separate access to flats. Harborne, Birmingham

Such a scheme proved to be about 14 per cent more expensive than a similar type of development of a flat site, but was adopted as the most economical solution on that particular location. It has proved to be a popular and successful estate. At a site in the same area, garages were placed beneath standard two-storey terraced housing, and although this added 7 per cent to the overall costs of each unit, a much greater density was possible. This cost differential is borne out by work at the Building Research Establishment. Their current paper 4/78 estimates that for various three-bedroom, five-person houses on a slope of 8° (1 in 7) the extra cost for basement construction amounted to between 8 and 11 per cent of the total. The ground area occupied by the houses however was reduced by about 30 per cent compared with other two-storey houses of similar size (Hodgkinson 1981f).

Bovis Homes generally estimate that the 'on costs' of adapted dwellings are 2–3 per cent above normal, but in many instances these houses on sloping sites are more attractive to purchasers than the more usual flat site houses. It is difficult to assess the hidden extras such as increased design, administrative and construction costs, but the small increase in building costs would appear to be commercially viable. The firm's disinclination to develop split level designs is perhaps partially attributable to costs and savings in external works. Normally

Fig. 4.21 Houses at Ulverston, Cumbria: view looking from downslope side. The houses take advantage of an 11° (1 : 5) slope to gain views across Morecambe Bay to the Bowland Forest and North Yorkshire Moors. Entrance is on the upslope side from the back of the site. The houses have integral garages and 'first floor' reception rooms. The earth is retained at the back of each house, but otherwise there is little that is of non-standard construction

Fig. 4.22 Houses at Ulverston, Cumbria. View looking from upslope side of houses in Fig. 4.21

Fig. 4.23 These private houses on a relatively steeply sloping site at Ambleside, Cumbria, place the service areas at a lower level. The views to the fells from the upper levels are magnificent, but vehicular access down the slope is somewhat tortuous

Fig. 4.24 The individually-designed house on the larger plot can select the most advantageous position to avoid the more extreme slopes, yet also take advantage of the gradient to gain prospect, and hide away the motor car (Private house, Ambleside, Cumbria)

Fig. 4.25 A block of flats has been sliced in half to match the ground levels. Woodgate Valley, Birmingham

only 2 per cent of building costs are spent by Bovis on externals, a figure which rises to 3 per cent on sloping sites. The following section will show that split levels accommodated within the dwelling can result in considerable savings on external earth manipulation and retention, though, as the Bovis figures for these elements are low, savings would be correspondingly minimal.

Split level dwellings

Variations in the number and disposition of the floors within a single dwelling can often produce a house of irregular form, hence its suitability for detached dwellings. Within this section, 'split level' is used to describe a type of house in which changes of level are usually of half a storey height and occur within an external envelope and plan form which are often quite regular although the section may have a staggered profile.

Development of such forms can result in both an increase of fees for design, estimating and site supervision and also more intricate (and therefore more costly) construction. The split level section can create difficulties with constructing and weatherproofing the groundworks, complications with the bearing of intermediate floors and idiosyncratic roof design. Some of these features may, however, be desired on grounds other than cost. By keeping the building profile as close as possible to the natural lie of the land (which split level designs allow)

Fig. 4.26 Split level house on quite a modest slope at Darwen, Lancashire. Most modern housing shows a reluctance to use an inclined ridge line (compare Figs 3.25 and 4.12)

Fig. 4.27 Split-level housing at Primrose Hill, Birmingham, follows the line of the sloping site

Fig. 4.28 The split level section is clearly visible on the end elevation (Primrose Hill, Birmingham)

substantial savings are made in the external works. Split level forms have certainly appeared workable to several local authorities who employ staff with sufficient scope to explore and exploit the full possibilities of these forms.

Primrose Hill, Birmingham

During the 1960s the City of Birmingham had an impressive record of house building. The five major redevelopment areas in the inner city were under construction, followed by the vast estates at Castle Vale and Chelmsley Wood. Extensive use was made of industrialized building methods for both high and low rise blocks, and the majority of the houses were on flat greenfield sites. In the following decade the pace of development slowed, available sites were mostly smaller or more difficult to plan. Design became less regimented in layout, smaller in scale and more human in detail.

The topography of the south and south-west fringes of the city where much recent building has taken place is relatively hilly and this has led to a number of interesting schemes. In the Woodgate Valley, an elbow unit was devised to allow development to meander along the contour. At Woodgate and elsewhere, standard flat site two-storey houses were also adapted to allow an integral garage and front entrance to be planned a complete storey height beneath the normal ground level. Terraces of standard houses have also been stepped and staggered to follow the site contours, but specially designed houses have occasionally been built on slopes of up to 14° (1 in 4). A recent scheme at Primrose Hill comprises 26 houses, 12 flats and 6 bungalows built along and partially down the contours of a north-west facing slope of 8° (1 in 7). The gradient did not need such a radical solution as that for Frankley (see below). The flats and bungalows were modified from standard designs but special split level units of relatively narrow frontage

(4.5 m) but 9 m depth were developed for the two- and three-bedroom houses. The living area is half a level below the kitchen/dining area with bedrooms above both levels. The bathroom is placed in the centre of the upper levels, lit by a slot window where the roof line steps to follow the ground slope. The superstructure costs of these special houses was 17 per cent more expensive than equivalent two-storey houses of more conventional design, the bungalows 7 per cent more expensive and the flats 4 per cent.

Such costs compare quite favourably, however, with an aged persons' housing scheme of twenty three dwellings on a sloping site at North Road, Harborne. This scheme went to tender four months before that of the special units at Frankley but the Harborne project used standard units then available, modified by stepping to the gradient. This housing is typical of the care for detailing and sensitive landscaping of Birmingham's recent developments. The difficulties of ground slope and conditions (the gradient is 5.4° (1 in 10) and faces north) made necessary *ad hocs* 14 per cent above Housing Cost Yardstick to adapt these otherwise normal units.

St Ann's, Nottingham

Housing designed for a sloping site in the St Ann's district of Nottingham by the John Stedman Design Group makes it possible to compare the costs of overcoming slope by external works and by split level housing. One-, two- and three-storey dwellings for the City of Nottingham were designed in two separate contracts. The first phase (St Ann's A, tender date April 1974) consisted of 168 units built at a density of 188 bedspaces per hectare at the southern end of the

Fig. 4.29 Old persons' housing at North Road, Harborne (Birmingham)

sloping site. This development contained no specially designed units. The problems of slope were overcome in the external works. St Ann's B followed (tender date, September 1974) and contained 174 dwellings at 182 bedspaces per hectare. In this second phase, a specially designed split-level, three-bedroom, five-person house formed nearly half the development.

A comparison of the two contracts reveals the anomalies which exist even between two similar projects and which make accurate analysis so difficult. The split level units were more expensive in strict building terms than the equivalent houses built on the flat, but when site development works are taken into account the position is reversed. Substructure costs for the split level units were almost twice the costs of those for the conventional units. Superstructure costs were similar but the proportion of site development costs for the conventional units was nearly three times those for the split level dwellings.

In the conventional three-bedroom, five-person units, substructure costs account for less than 10 per cent of the building costs within the perimeter; the same figure for the split level houses is 15 per cent. When site development costs are considered, substructures on the conventional house drop to 7 per cent and to 14 per cent on the split level units. Overall, however, the split level units were about 8 per cent cheaper than the equivalent conventional house on Site A.

These figures show how the apparently extra expense of specially designed dwellings can be offset by other savings, particularly in site development costs. On Site B, which contains the split level houses, most of the problems of slope were solved within the perimeter of the dwelling. On the earlier scheme, much more money was spent in overcoming the slope by external works.

Fig. 4.30 Split level houses at St Ann's, Nottingham (scheme B) were 8 per cent cheaper than similar houses nearby which were accommodated by cut-and-fill. Cheverton Court in the background

Redditch

Walkwood 14 is an estate of sixty seven houses of traditional construction developed at a density of 171 bedspaces per hectare about 3 km (2 miles) south of the town centre. Tenders were received in August 1979, the lowest being just over £1 million. The land slopes 8 m from north-west to south-east, creating a slope of up to 7° (1 in 8). The majority of units are standard two-storey construction with the slope accommodated by steps and staggers in the houses and retained landscape works. At the maximum slope, a three-bedroom, five-person house has been adapted to a split level section with two terraces. It also steps and staggers across the contour.

Fig. 4.31 Redditch: Walkwood 14. Three-bedroom, five-person, split level housing

Compared with the more standard three-bedroom, five-person unit built elsewhere on the site, the split level verson is 2 per cent smaller in area but cost, at tender, 3 per cent more. At that time, the greater costs were due to the superstructure being 4 per cent higher.

Stepping and staggering has been used across most of the rest of the site; the nine terraces contain twenty steps with staggers and three staggers without steps. At a sum of nearly £1,000 each (third quarter 1979), this cost was greater than the difference between the 'standard' and split level dwellings.

An *ad hoc* of nearly £14,000 (1.5 per cent) was obtained on this scheme because of the slope. Two thirds of this was for earth moving and retaining *within* the perimeter of the dwellings. The remainder was for similar site works externally.

These three case studies therefore show a tendency for superstructure costs for split level dwellings to be higher than for conventional designs. Perhaps more significant were that substructure costs could be up to twice as much for split level houses. However, this could be offset by external works which could be as much as three times more expensive for construction using cut-and-fill. Overall, the cost differences were not great. Some private sector developers however have expressed, verbally, that they are reluctant to use split level forms due to design costs and uncertainty about whether they will sell. On the other hand, an estate by a large housing contractor for Cwmbran Development Corporation did not bear this fear out.

Many sites in the South Wales Valleys have extreme conditions of slope. A development of 171 dwellings at Cwmbran (tender date December 1974) included a stipulation for split level designs in the Development Corporation's brief. It would indeed have been extremely difficult to adapt the contours to suit more normal house types as the average gradient was about 9° (1 in 6).

This tender was based on traditional masonry superstructure but was eventually carried out in timber-framed construction which had considerable advantages in saving time. Substructure costs were 9.2 per cent of total construction costs (excluding preliminaries), as against the same company's traditional flat site dwellings which had a substructure percentage of 7.2 per cent. At the time this 2 per cent extra for the split level form amounted to about £200 per dwelling – considerably less than it would have cost to terrace the hillside into flat shelves.

The most common 'split' is 1.2 m (4 ft). There are twelve variations of step and stagger throughout the estate. The total extra construction cost for the non-standard substructure was only about 1.3 per cent. More than three times this amount was ultimately saved by adopting the timber framed superstructures.

Some American experiences
In North America, where private houses tend to be larger than in Britain with a tradition of building part of the home into the ground, even on flat sites, it is not

Fig. 4.32 Split level housing on slope of 9 ° (1 : 6) at Cwmbran, Gwent. Note the asymmetrical roof pitch, and brick skin concealing timber framed construction

(a)

(b)

(c)

Fig. 4.33a, b, c, d Small blocks of split level flats show the advantage of using sloping sites for higher density housing: less ground is disturbed in proportion to the number of persons accommodated. These otherwise quite ordinary blocks in Kendal, Cumbria, sensitively retain the scale and character of a valley-side site, close to the amenities of the town centre. Architect: Sir Frederick Gibberd and Partners

114

(d)

surprising to find a greater willingness to experiment with varying forms of hillside housing. Many schemes there, especially on the affluent West Coast, seek inspiration from difficult sites to create special designs to exploit the setting. The extra construction costs seem to be quite easily balanced by lower land costs for awkward sites and the sales potential of interesting homes.

One of two Award of Merit winners in the 1979 'Homes for Better Living' programme was for an 11 ha (27 acre) complex of shingle clad town houses in Walnut Creek, California. One hundred and sixty-one units were arranged along and in cul-de-sacs off a loop road which follows the contours of the rolling land. A majority of the units have open views to the distant hills to the east and west. To overcome and exploit the slope, four basic types were developed. Some of these have split level sections, others a full storey height and minor changes of level within individual floors. With areas of 155 m^2 to 235 m^2 the houses are large by most standards. They are of a size which allows scope for more individual planning. Prices per unit area are comparable with the larger private houses in the UK.

In the uphill design, bedrooms are on the lower level. Above, all living space is treated as 'one large skylit room' to make the most of the views. In the downhill unit there is an immediate view on entry across the stepdown living room and raised dining room ('How to tackle a Hillside Site' *Housing*, New York 1979).

115

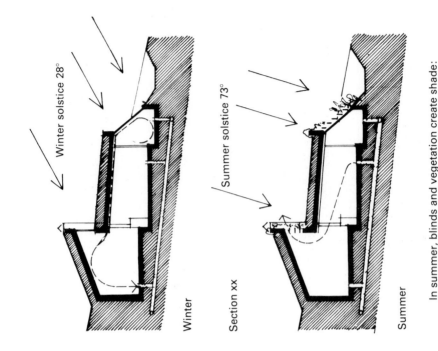

Winter solstice 28°

Winter

Section xx

Summer solstice 73°

Summer

In summer, blinds and vegetation create shade: warm air is extracted at high level

In winter, warm air circulates throughout the house the earth insulates at all seasons

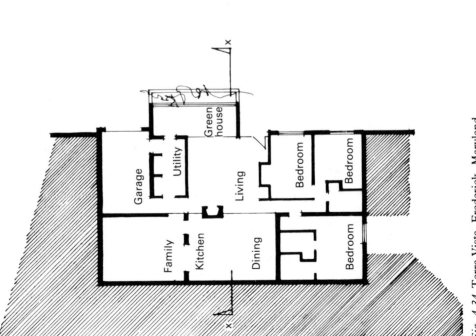

Garage

Utility

Green house

Living

Bedroom

Bedroom

Family

Kitchen

Dining

Bedroom

Fig. 4.34 Terra Vista, Frederick, Maryland

Fig. 4.35 Public sector housing at Kate's Hill, Dudley, West Midlands. Much of this site has a gradient of 15°–20° and the local council has considered both house designs and layouts very carefully to fit this physically awkward site. Several modifications to house designs including extra storeys downslope and extra masonry have been used to avoid large amounts of earth modelling

Fig. 4.36 Kate's Hill, Dudley. The steep site has been used to achieve a sense of drama in the design of these public sector houses as well as to take advantage of sunlight and commanding views. Some of the intervening spaces, however, do feel cold and uninviting, perhaps inevitably at such high density

Fig. 4.37 Kate's Hill, Dudley. Some earth modelling and retention has been inevitable, largely to accommodate vehicles on-site

Two further schemes in California illustrate the Americans' acceptance of non-standard designs. At Big Canyon, Newport Beach, clusters of town houses were constructed above underground garaging built into the slope. This added about 10 per cent to the cost of each unit but preserved views and increased density. A variety of sizes, plan types and cross sectional ideas were employed. A site at Turtle Rock Glen had a gradient of 12° (1 in 4.5). Semi-detached units were used to minimize regrading, each house being designed around a split level section.

Commentators in the USA tend to differentiate their hillside housing into downhill and uphill categories, depending on the point of entry. Downhill units can take advantage of dramatic views from the point of entry through the house to a distant prospect. Uphill houses, stepping up the contour, can overcome natural siting problems. The Americans obviously believe that hillside housing offers great sales potential which is more easily maximized in downhill solutions.

Cascade or stepped hill housing

Where gradients are as steep as 11° (1 in 5) or steeper it is increasingly difficult to place housing upon them except for specially designed forms. On such slopes one of the most common answers is to provide a section which resembles a chest of drawers, with each 'drawer' pulled out further as the building follows down the slope. Above ground, each storey is supported partly by the one below and partly by the ground. If the building is subdivided horizontally into individual

118

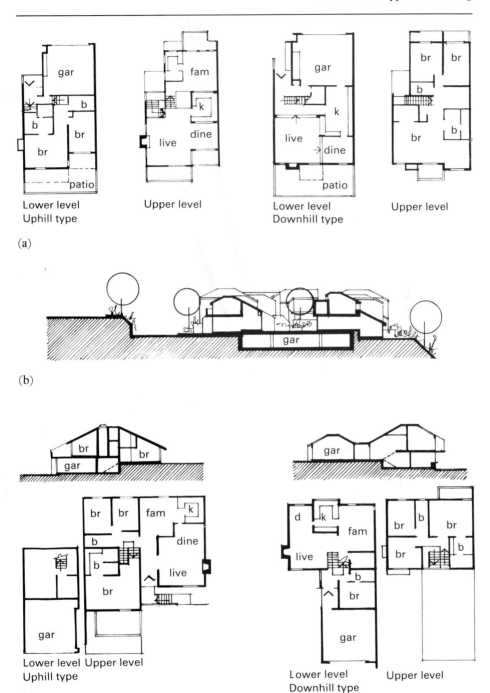

Fig. 4.38 (a) Walnut Creek, California (b) Big Canyon, California; (c) Turtle Rock Glen, California.

dwellings, this building form resembles a block of flats (see Crawford 1975, pp 170–81 and Gibberd 1962, p 291).

Frankley

The Frankley scheme developed by Birmingham City Council on the south-western outskirts of the city consists of two parallel chains of sixty-one three-storey terraced houses each with integral garage. The long, sloping roof at 39° to the horizontal allows some summer sunlight to enter through 'Velux' rooflights. The main living areas on the middle level have gardens on the south

Fig. 4.39 Birmingham City Council housing at Frankley. The brief comprised nineteen bungalows, and sixty-one specially designed family houses of two, three and four bedrooms with integral garages.

Fig. 4.40 Birmingham City Council housing at Frankley. Most of this consists of: ground floor – garage, entrance, kitchen; first floor – living room, bedroom; second floor – one or two bedrooms. Some of the site is as steep as 15° (1 in 4)

side. The stepped foundation profile was designed to eliminate the possibility of water penetration.

The cost of such a solution is bound to be increased by the measures necessary to overcome inherent site difficulties and these one-off houses were approximately 15 per cent more expensive than contemporary units of similar size and standard design (Figs. 4.39 and 4.40; see also Figs 3.19, 3.31, 3.32, 3.33, 3.34 and 3.41).

Cheverton Court, St Ann's District of Nottingham   (Davies, Wythe and Eley 1978). The site comprises 0.747 ha south of Cranmer Street, Nottingham, on a steep, south-facing slope overlooking the city centre about one kilometre away. There is a fall of 17 m in 80 m, but much of the site is steeper than this would suggest. The 45° slope of the roofs (Fig. 4.41) generally follows the natural ground line.

Fig. 4.41 Cheverton Court, St Ann's, Nottingham. The 45° pitch of the roof follows the natural ground slope

Fig. 4.42 Cheverton Court, Nottingham. The steepness of the site would probably make it unsuitable for the elderly

Most of the site is composed of easily excavated Bunter Sandstone overlain by a stiff reddish brown Keuper Marl. The site is well drained, which helped construction.

The scheme, designed by John Wythe and Roger Stone of the John Stedman Design Group, comprises fifty-nine one-person bedsits of 25 m², forty-seven one-person flats of 32.5 m², twenty-one two-person flats and maisonettes from 46.5 m² and two three-person maisonettes. At the highest point, the scheme extends up to nine storeys, though most of the units have their entrance at 'ground' level. There are three access levels and a maximum of two flights of stairs up or down to each unit. Being largely for single people and young couples, the stepped access is not as great a problem as it might otherwise have been. The fire officer however treated it as a nine-storey block of flats and special means of escape were needed.

For a total floor area of 5,504 m², total scheme costs were £207/m² (at tender, 7 August 1975). This was made up as follows:

	per cent
Works below lowest floor finish	14.19
Structural elements	29.51
Finishes and fittings	10.32
Services	16.31
Preliminaries and insurance	10.62
Contingencies	2.05
External works	17.00

Fig. 4.43 Cheverton Court, St Ann's, Nottingham; landscaping and amenity area for residents

This of course omits professional fees, land acquisition and legal costs, which according to the National Building Agency (1976) might typically comprise 23 per cent of total house construction costs. It is, of course, very dangerous to draw comparisons due to the special nature of the scheme at Nottingham and differences in definitions.

At the time of construction the scheme was about 37 per cent above the Housing Cost Yardstick basic allowances. Approximately half of this was due to site development costs and half due to the filling of old basements, excavation and reinforced concrete forming part of the fabric of each dwelling. The reinforced concrete forms steps in the floor slabs and the back walls of the dwellings which also act as retaining walls.

123

Fig. 4.44 Cheverton Court, St Ann's, Nottingham. Garaging tucked away beneath the main structure almost out of sight

The superstructure, which is not abnormally expensive, is of traditional brick and block cavity construction. The roof is of preconstructed softwood trusses. Servicing costs were also not abnormally high despite including 6.71 per cent of the total construction costs plus external works on the high pressure district heating system. No gas supply was provided.

It would seem therefore that most of the abnormal costs of this ingenious solution to housing on a very steep slope were due to site preparation and substructure. In purely economic terms such solutions would probably be viable only in relatively fashionable districts or where there are benefits such as fine views.

Redditch Oakenshaw 5

Oakenshaw 5 is a mixed estate of 3.53 hr (8.5 acres) on an attractive but topographically challenging site 2 km (1.5 miles) south of the town centre. The land slopes nearly 30 m (100 ft) from west to east with gradients of 11° (1 in 5). The layout divides into three distinct areas. To the south-east, a cluster of stepped and staggered short terraces of single family dwellings; on the north-east, a long crescent of sixteen larger houses hugs the contour (Fig. 4.45) and to the west a series of blocks of flats and maisonettes cascades down the steepest part of the site (Figs. 4.46 to 4.48).

At tender stage (early 1979) there was to be fifteen of these blocks, but extreme difficulties with the sandy ground caused three of them to be omitted. The form

Fig. 4.45 Redditch: Oakenshaw 5. A long terrace of sixteen houses hugs the contour. Note also the broken roof line in contrast to Figs 3.25 and 4.12

and content of these very special units is more akin to St Ann's (Cheverton Court) than the Frankley project on the outskirts of Birmingham. The Redditch units are flats and maisonettes on two and three staggered levels, not individual terraced dwellings of three or four floors.

These flats at Oakenshaw take up only 40 per cent of the bedspaces of the original layout of the estate, but their cost was 57 per cent of the building tender figure. The Development Corporation received an *ad hoc* allowance for the whole project of over £111,000 within a total of £1.7 million. Nearly half of the *ad hocs* was to overcome the particular difficulties of the external works, but almost £32,000 helped offset the costs of foundations to the flats. £12,000 was needed to provide suspended rather than solid ground floors and the unstable ground conditions made necessary a further £7,500 for foundation work. The substructure element of the special flats was 14 per cent of their total cost and the four-person maisonettes in these blocks were 25 per cent more expensive than an equivalent house elsewhere on the estate.

It would have been impossible however to develop the western area of Oakenshaw 5 with a more standard dwelling type. The imaginative design to overcome difficult conditions certainly has considerable interest, charm and ingenuity which helps compensate for the expense involved.

Fig. 4.46 Redditch, Oakenshaw 5. A series of flat blocks cascades down a slope of about 11° (1 in 5)

Fig. 4.47 Redditch, Oakenshaw 5. Each dwelling has an entrance at ground floor level

Fig. 4.48 Redditch, Oakenshaw 5. Top of a block of flats

The Cefn Isaf scheme, Cefn-coed-y-cymmer, Breconshire
Designed by J R Gammon, H O Williams and Associates for Vaynor and Penderyn Rural District Council in the mid 1960s (Gammon and Thompson 1970), this scheme of thirty-four flats (21 × 2 person, 2 × 3, 9 × 4 and 2 × 5) occupies two-thirds of an acre on a south-facing slope of up to 22° (1 in 2.5) in parts. Fourteen dwellings are contained in a three-storey block linked by footbridges to a five-storey block downslope, containing twenty dwellings. The storeys of this block are set 2.13 m over the storey below, providing every flat with a terrace across the whole frontage. Covered walkways have been formed between the hillside and the rear walls of the flats in the lower block giving access directly from ground level, providing ducts for services and avoiding tanking against the retained ground.

The site is a difficult one, not only due to a 10 m drop in level but because of ground conditions partly of running sand and ironstone needing excavation elsewhere. The construction is of traditional brick walls and *in situ* concrete floors with timber frames built off concrete cross beams supported on concrete piles. Cavity party walls, floating timber floors on glass fibre quilt and laminated polyurethane ceiling panels provide good sound and heat insulation. All the flats are centrally heated, half by gas, half by electricity.

127

The scheme costs were made up as follows:

	Per cent
Work below lowest floor finish	17.11
Structural elements	44.26
Finishes and fittings	11.12
Services	14.42
Preliminaries and insurance	4.43
External works	8.66

The high cost of below lowest floor finish clearly reflects the difficult ground conditions and slope. In the three-storey block, 42 × 43 cm diameter piles were used, averaging 7.3 m in length to support a concrete retaining wall 2.6 m in height and 23 cm thick. Another retaining wall of the same thickness and 2.13 m in height was also necessary. The five-storey block needed 20 × 43 cm diameter piles, average length 4.9 m, supporting two retaining walls of 23 cm thickness and each 2.6 m in height. *In situ* reinforced concrete ribs built on rock formation level at an average depth of 2.74 m below level 1 supported another retaining wall 2.28 m in height and 23 cm thick. Part of the upper floor costs would be due to the access bridges and suspended ground floors.

External works included the cost of widening and regrading one of the streets on the boundary of the site. Although the scheme was started before the introduction of the Housing Cost Yardstick in December 1968, the areas provided and standards were related to Parker Morris Standards.

In Britain to date, the 'chest of drawers' has been applied on only a limited scale and usually for steep slopes of about 20° to 40° (about 1 in 3 to almost 1 in 1). The principle can, however, be used over a wider range of slopes and for a variety of floor arrangements and site layouts. The results of a reserarch project carried out at the University of Karlsruhe are reported in Bensemann (1974). Four basic floor plans (wide frontage, narrow frontage, L shaped and T shaped) and the ways these may be adapted over slopes of about 8° to 41° (1 in 7 to almost 1 in 1) are explained including the effects on privacy, sightlines and internal arrangements including the need for artificial lighting and ventilation. The T and L shaped plans were found to have a maximum useful depth of 10 m compared with 7.5 m for other forms.

At a gradient of about 15° (1 in 4), the 'chest of drawers' becomes fully extended, the back wall of one unit being in the same vertical plane as the front wall of the next. On gentler slopes the blocks are separated or the floor of each unit is dropped below the level of the roof of the one below, thereby increasing privacy. On steeper gradients, the dwellings overlap more and more, affecting daylighting and ventilation to different degrees depending on floor layouts as well as angle of slope.

The chest of drawers principle can also be used on flat sites to give a sense of identity, individuality and improve views from groups of flats. At Evry near Paris, the principle has been used to form what is basically a pyramid with traffic penetration right into the middle of the grouping underneath the upper floors (Simounet 1982).

Fig. 4.49 Paris. In France, the 'chest of drawers' principle on flat sites is common

Fig. 4.50 The 'chest of drawers' principle on gently undulating ground at Créteil, Paris

Where the gradient of the site makes it a viable alternative, the cascade form offers perhaps the most interesting solution to housing on steep slopes. It can create relatively intense development, without either the claustrophobic quality of some high-density low-rise schemes on flat sites or divorcing living quarters from the ground as suffered in high-rise flats. The profile keeps close to the natural slope and so helps the building to integrate with its immediate landscape. The stepped profile can provide clear, unobstructed views without loss of privacy. It is hardly surprising that it is a favoured form with those seeking to exploit the full potential of sloping sites where the land is to be used intensively.

Handled thoughtfully, as shown in the scheme for holiday homes at Looe in Cornwall by architect Michael Deakin, the cascade solution need not be the preserve of those working with government subsidy or where expense is not important. The original layout aimed to produce 192 units on the 2.6 ha site at

129

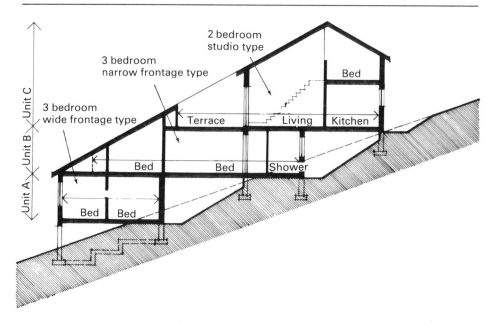

Fig. 4.51 Project for Holiday Village in Cornwall. Cascade section of houses on posts. Architect: Michael Deakin

Fig. 4.52 At Givors (20 km south of Lyon, France) these highly individual, organic, cascade forms climb up this hillside at a gradient of over 25 ° in parts and overlook the centre of this small town. On the ground floor, shops, a new library and other community facilities are part of the structure. This photograph was taken from the main square in the centre of Givors

Fig. 4.53 Givors: Each unit, different from the others, has its own small, suspended garden. Design was by Jean Renaudie and Cabinet Etra.

the relatively high density of 235 bedspaces per hectare. No vehicular access penetrated the steeply sloping setting which has average gradients around 18° (1 in 3). Selling prices (1982) of £11,500 for a one-bedroom unit of 34 m^2 and £17,500 for a three-bedroom dwelling of 72 m^2 were comparable in size and cost with the houses on the Arden Estate at Banbury, although the homes at Looe, being temporary residences, were modestly furnished and equipped. Reference to the typical section (Fig. 4.51) shows that the dwellings have been kept on or above the ground rather than cut into the slope. In this respect they share certain characteristics with the next house type to be identified, those raised on posts.

131

Fig. 4.54 Givors. The hot dry climate has clearly influenced design. Due to unstable ground conditions these dwellings have been built on piles. This led to financial problems particularly as they are let at controlled rents

Houses raised on posts

Rather than mould the site by earthworks, the ground floor level can be determined by reference to the highest point on the ground where the house is to be built and the rest of the house raised on posts resting on concrete pier foundations. This is a cheap and easy solution where lightweight construction is to be used. It is a form used by many individual beach houses and holiday homes and was the method chosen for self-build schemes designed by Walter Segal and Jon Broome at Forest Hill, Sydenham, and Bromley in the London Borough of Lewisham (Ellis 1980). The system of timber framed construction is a development of the simple 'one-off' houses designed by Segal for private clients in the late 1960s, such as that at Halstead, Essex, applied to mass housing.

Fig. 4.55 Givors: plenty of shade has been created; important in summer here

To enable the Council to get benefits of loan sanction and subsidy from the Department of the Environment the houses were built as Council houses, the future occupiers being contracted to build them. When complete, the self-builders were granted ninety-nine year leases and a Council mortgage on 50 per cent of the valuation minus an estimate of the value of their labour. 50 per cent therefore remained in Council ownership and a rent was charged, though the occupiers have been given the option of gradually increasing their share up to 100 per cent. Twelve houses of eight different types were built on four sites. The modular form of construction helped to achieve variety of form and close adaptation to ground conditions including slope.

At March 1978 prices, the cost per square metre was £218 (Bromley), £224 and £230 for the two sites in Sydenham and £251 at Forest Hill. The most expensive houses at Forest Hill were on a difficult clay site which had such severe drainage problems that it was reported (Ellis 1980) that the Council had no hope of getting

133

Fig. 4.56 Givors: Many of these dwellings offer a splendid
view over this small town. Yet they still retain a fair degree
of privacy for housing at such high density

Department of the Environment loan sanction for it. One of the two sites at
Sydenham was on made-up ground of clay, gravel, cinders and bricks over 2 m in
depth underlain by 4.4 m of stiff brown grey silty sandy clay (Claygate Beds) and
London Clay. It required foundations 3 m (10 ft) deep. The slope is 5° (1 in 11)
and facing north-north-east.

The other site at Sydenham has a natural spring and various overgrown
earthworks and faces north-north-east at a gradient of 6° (1 in 9). Generally the
costs, which inluded a notional allowance for labour, were considered to be only
about half of some comparable schemes in London at that time. One problem
however could be that of energy costs. These detached houses are exposed to
atmospheric heat losses on all six sides, though insulation seems to have reduced
heat losses to below those of some conventional houses.

Fig. 4.57 Private housing at Halstead, Essex: Early (1968)
design of Walter Segal's 'house raised on posts'

Technical factors influencing choice of design

Problems of adapting house design

The reluctance of many developers to employ special house types adapted to slope
compared with their apparent willingness to spend large sums in manipulation of
slopes to accommodate flat site designs, can be appreciated by examining some of
the technical issues which arise.

The possibility of differential settlement in a structure of differing levels and
other footing problems associated with the bearing capacity of the soil can make
specially engineered foundations necessary. If part of the usable volume of the
house is below the normal level of the damp proof course (150 mm above adjacent
ground), waterproofing will be required. Once out of the ground, difficulties are
perhaps less acute, but partially exposed party and gable walls and awkward
junctions caused by changes of level or offsets on plan make thoughtful designing
of joints and junctions necessary. Potentially hazardous details like the insertion
of soakers, stepped cavity trays and flashings in those areas liable to moisture
penetration require careful supervision.

Fig. 4.58 Housing at Sydenham. The diagonal boarding
hides the open space beneath the raised 'ground' floor.

All housing developers, whether public or private, wish to minimize the
chance of inherent defects occurring after the dwellings have become occupied.
With special designs, especially those built on a mass scale with minimum
supervision, possibly with part of their structure cut into the ground, such
problems are more likely to occur and be more difficult to locate and rectify.

The Building Research Establishment has done much work on soils,
foundations and fill; see *Digests* numbered 63, 64, 67, 274 and 275. There is
certainly no hard and fast way of relating angle of slope to house design to be
adopted even for a given soil type. Variations in soil type, particularly the ratio of
sand : silt : clay influences the choice of design. In clay soils there is a greater
incentive to adapt design, whereas on sandy soils the site can be modified, being
more easily drained and generally easier to work.

Unless the scheme is a multi-storey development occupying the minimum ground area, the greater the density of any layout, the more critical the connection between the design of individual dwellings and ground form. Almost any design can be adapted to slope if the density is low, as there will be space to select the most advantageous setting and room to manipulate the natural contours. With higher densities, the proportion of land covered is greater and the ability to select and adapt the existing landscape becomes less easy.

Although it is not possible to predict with certainty the best solution for a given slope and soil type, there is a tendency for each design to be desirable over a range of gradients, this range varying according to soil type. A study of Cumbernauld (Denton 1963) emphasized the need to vary house designs according to ground conditions. Gentler slopes were developed with three-storey, six-person, narrow-fronted terraced houses diagonal to the contours. On slopes of between 4° and 2.5° (1 in 14 and 1 in 20) stepped terraces of two-storey houses were built normally or diagonally to the contours. On the steeper parts, split level houses in terraces parallel to the contours were built, stepped and staggered to provide diagonal pedestrian access with easier gradients.

Constructing dwellings to slopes is naturally more difficult than building on flat land. Not only may the form of the dwelling be special but the process of setting up and servicing the site itself can create complexities of access and difficulties with the placing of mechanical plant.

The complications of constructing cascade type structures or of even building part of a single dwelling can cause obvious difficulties of construction, most especially waterproofing. Even simple means of adaptation such as stepping and staggering blocks make for difficulities. Special care must be taken with foundations and, out of the ground, offset and exposed party walls require stepped flashing and cavity trays which, unless placed correctly, can lead to moisture penetration. Historically, such a problem was often avoided by placing the roof over a terrace block parallel with the slope of the ground (see for example, Figs. 3.25 and 4.12). The difficulties of short steps were thus overcome (Figs. 4.8 and 4.26 for example).

Guidance and remedies

In the *Registered House Builders Handbook* (Part II) (Revised in 1974), the National House Building Council lays down 'requirements' to cover all contingencies which the builder is likely to face. Requirement No. 5, 'Structural Design for Special Conditions', is, by its universal nature, somewhat bland, but requires the developer to comply with all relevant Codes of Practice and employ suitably qualified professionals to carry out the technical design. It also requires the builder to 'issue clear instructions for site personnel and not permit departure from the design without the designer's written consent'.

The *Handbook* contains a number of clauses covering precautions to be taken to overcome ground hazards. Clause 3, p. 22, lists such hazards as high water table, sulphates, peat, mines and mineral workings, made up ground, trees, low bearing capacity, adjacent buildings and existing drains. All these factors can be exacerbated on sloping ground.

Clause 23, p. 27 deals with specially designed foundations and states that anything other than standard strip foundations should be specially designed in accordance with Requirement No. 5. Stepped foundations can be used, so long as the overlap at each step is 300 mm or more and equal or greater to twice the thickness of the footing. If the depth of each step is greater than the thickness of the footing then Requirement No. 5 must be followed.

Paragraph 39 is of special importance to sloping sites, as it considers damp proofing of habitable areas below ground. Under the general dictate that 'the structure shall be impervious' it says that some method of tanking shall be employed and lists six rules for its use:

1. Vertical tanking to be separated from the inside of the structure by a minimum of 100 mm of solid construction.
2. If asphalt is used it is to be 20 mm thick on vertical surfaces and 30 mm thick on horizontal surfaces.
3. If polythene is used it is to be of at least 500 gauge with joints welded or properly lapped.
4. Tanking other than asphalt to follow Requirement 2(e).
5. Horizontal tanking more than 750 mm below ground level to be separated from the inside by a minimum of 100 mm of solid construction.
6. Tanking in damp-proof membranes, slabs, oversites and walls to be linked together to form an impervious structure.

It is as well to point out that beyond the guidance of this particular handbook there is some debate in the building industry as to the best methods of constructing waterproof basements. There is even a case for the use of reinforced concrete alone without tanking. Where basements are in concrete, the cost per square metre does not increase with depth up to 4.6 m where damp proof requirements are constant (RICS Design/Cost Research Working Party 1965). The additional cost of waterproofing concrete is relatively small and worthwhile where conditions do not justify asphalt tanking but should the structure crack, even minimally, water will not be withheld.

Asphalt tanking adds perhaps 15–20 per cent to costs and becomes brittle with age. It may also crack on settlement. Leaks in tanking can be difficult to trace, showing far from the source. On the other hand, tanking provides some protection against chemical attack and some contractors insist that it be done. For dry sites, a slab on plastic damp proof membrane and a painted damp proof membrane or adhesive sheet on external walls may be adequate (Hodgkinson 1981f).

Another problem where the floor level is considerably below the water table is the upward pressure of water on the floor. This may necessitate added load such as mass concrete (Hodgkinson 1981d). Chemicals in the water may have electrolytic or corrosive effects on piling and other structural elements and utilities. Sulphates may attack mortar in brickwork. Building Research

Establishment Digests 89 and 174 make recommendations on mortar, bricks and concrete resistance. Hodgkinson (1981c and d) recommends wrapping foundations in an inert protective layer such as polythene sheet.

It is also of considerable benefit to keep ground water away from basements and other areas built into the soil. The greatest difficulty from water seepage in retained structures of this scale is through a building up of hydrostatic pressure behind the retaining wall. This danger can be greatly reduced by using well-drained base fill material and land drainage to the outside. Wetness of the soil also influences heat losses (see below).

Fig. 4.59 Even on quite gentle slopes advantage is taken of thermal insulation properties of the ground. Hässelby, Stockholm

Energy, earth shelter and architectural form

Initial considerations

The most fundamental requirement of a building is its capacity to provide shelter and for its external envelope to act as a filter between the conditions of comfort required within and the potentially hostile environment without. The majority of housing therefore requires energy, either in the form of heat or cooling to maintain this balance. P A Stone estimates costs-in-use for 'typical houses' (at 5 per cent net discount rate) as follows: initial costs 56 per cent, maintenance 16 per cent fuel and attendance for heating and lighting 28 per cent (Stone 1980).

In recent years the crisis in the supply and the cost of fossil fuels has been coupled with uncertainty surrounding the viability of alternative sources of

Fig. 4.60 Rooms partly underground are very common in Swedish housing. Hässelby, Stockholm

Fig. 4.61 Rather than excavate the earth to create a flat platform, it is common in many countries to build up the earth on a gentle slope to give shelter. This house at Avallon in central France has two storeys, including integral garage on the downslope side

Fig. 4.62 Earth shelter for ground floor flats with direct access to maisonettes above. Cergy Pontoise near Paris

energy and the cost effectiveness of passive systems such as solar power and the safety of nuclear power. There has, therefore, been greater emphasis on the capacity of the building envelope to provide more adequate insulation. In September 1981 the Building Regulations of the United Kingdom increased the 'deemed to satisfy' requirements in dwellings by almost 50 per cent over the existing 1976 figures. (The Building (Second Amendment) Regulations 1981 increased the maximum U value of the external wall element to 0.6 $W/m^{2\circ}$ C from 1.0 $W/m^{2\circ}/C$ and roofs to a maximum of 0.35 $W/m^{2\circ}$ C from 0.6 $W/m^{2\circ}$ C.) Other more northerly countries have had higher standards for many years.

The flow of energy from a structure is primarily dependent on the amount of ventilation that is allowed to pass through it and the heat transmissions of the envelope itself. Ventilation is largely independent of slope and in fact in any building the control of draughts is one of the most effective means of energy conservation.

Thermal transmittance is a complex science and has been the focus of much research at the Building Research Establishment and by engineers. In general terms, the flow of energy through the fabric is dependent upon the form and physical characteristics of the envelope, the difference between the inside and outside temperatures and the degree of exposure of the building within its setting. Physical characteristics will include the ability of the envelope to act as an insulator, including its capacity to absorb or repel moisture.

The total heat flow through any element of given construction is the heat flow per unit area multiplied by the area of that element (cf. R W R Muncey 1979, p 17). Assuming that in any given type of housing, elements of construction will conform to similar standards, it can be seen that the smaller the surface area of the envelope, the more efficient the form as an energy conserver. B Givoni has also deduced that the greater the relative exterior area, the higher the potential heat loss per unit volume (Givoni 1976). This would seem to conclude that the most energy-efficient form is that of least surface area relative to enclosed volume. Hawkes (1981) however has concluded that energy use is not dependent on building shape within limits – low energy building is possible for many basic shapes.

Thus the dwelling within a square plan shape would appear to be a form with potential for energy conservation. For detached houses in cool climates built traditionally with small areas of glazing allowing little solar gain from radiation, this tends to be true. Taking into account, however, the total energy requirements throughout the year, including the advantages of solar gain, Victor Olgyay has tested a typical American house in four types of climate and concludes that a dwelling planned along an east–west axis is the most efficient. In a cold area, the ratio of north–south walls to east-west is most efficient at 1 : 1.1. For temperate zones, the ratio is 1 : 1.6, hot zones 1 : 1.3 (including the use of an internal courtyard for cooling) and in hot humid areas 1 : 1.7 (Olgyay 1963).

In damp temperate climates such as that of Britain there is less concern with achieving solar gain than with heat losses during winter. In a country too where houses are smaller in area than those in North America and with a large proportion in either semi-detached or terrace form it is sensible to keep external surfaces to a minimum. It should also be remembered that such is the complexity of heat transmittance from different parts of a dwelling that overall energy losses are not simply proportional to the exposed surface areas. In the present study however it is likely that the wide frontage adopted on the Arden Estate at Banbury, for example, will be potentially less energy efficient than that at the expensive but compact ski-slope profile at Cheverton Court, Nottingham. Housing on posts, such as those in south-east London, expose a large external surface relative to their plan area and need very effective heat insulation.

Housing on slopes offers both problems and possibilities to the energy-conscious designer. On a sloping site, any form of attached house is likely to have a greater part of its exterior skin exposed than a similar design on a flat site. This is due to the relative changes in level between adjacent dwellings. Housing forms which seek to follow the contours also have a larger area of external surface relative to plan area than more normal types. On the other hand, hillside housing offers potential to take advantage of the insulating properties of the soil by burying part of the structure into the ground and so reduce the extent of exposed surface area. Although such forms appear to offer exciting possibilities for energy conservation, their use in the British climate together with the traditions of the British building industry, makes them hardly viable. Indeed, the examples identified in this Guide which created forms to accommodate the slope, sought to keep the retained earth away from habitable rooms. The cascade houses at Frankley, Birmingham and Oakenshaw 5, Redditch, both involved creating voids between the ground and the rear walls of the housing. The scheme for holiday homes in Looe deliberately raised the structures out of the banking. With energy prices expected by some to rise faster than the general rate of inflation, attitudes may change.

Total heat flow into or out of a building is a product of thermal transmittance, area and temperature difference:

$$Q = UA (\theta_a - \theta_b)$$

	where Q	=	total heat flow
	U	=	thermal transmittance
	A	=	area of surface
	$\theta_a\theta_b$	=	temperatures inside and outsde

Special house designs for slope can influence all three of these factors which determine heat flow.

Temperature differences in buildings

Frequently, housing on slopes is more exposed to convectional heat losses than that on the level. Occasionally, as in a sheltered valley, the opposite may be the case. The flatter hill top may be more exposed and the flat valley floor may suffer from cold air drainage. These climatic effects of slope were discussed in Chapter 2.

Effects of slope on the exposed surface area

The reduction of surface area presented to the outside air and the saving in energy which such forms allow, can be used in the design of earth-sheltered housing on sloping sites. Of the total energy losses of the average British house, over 90 per cent is to the outside air through radiative cooling (36 per cent), air infiltration (38 per cent) and convection by cooling (18 per cent). Only about 8 per cent is lost to the ground by conduction.

It has already been mentioned that two of the major factors influencing the flow of heat from a building to or from the atmosphere are the insulating properties of the external envelope and its exposed surface area. Assuming comparable examples and similar levels of insulation (in many countries mandatory standards of insulation are imposed) and ignoring also the energy gains by solar radiation, it follows that where an input of energy is required to keep internal temperatures at an acceptable level the smaller the exposed surface area of the dwelling, the greater its energy conserving capacity.

Checks have been carried out on the range of examples of housing types explained in this Guide, calculating their surface areas and the proportion of that area exposed to the air, against comparable areas of dwellings on flat ground:

1. The wide frontage, shallow depth houses developed along the contours at the Arden Estate, Banbury, to minimize cut-and fill were 20 per cent greater in exposed surface area than similar sized but more standard terraced houses.

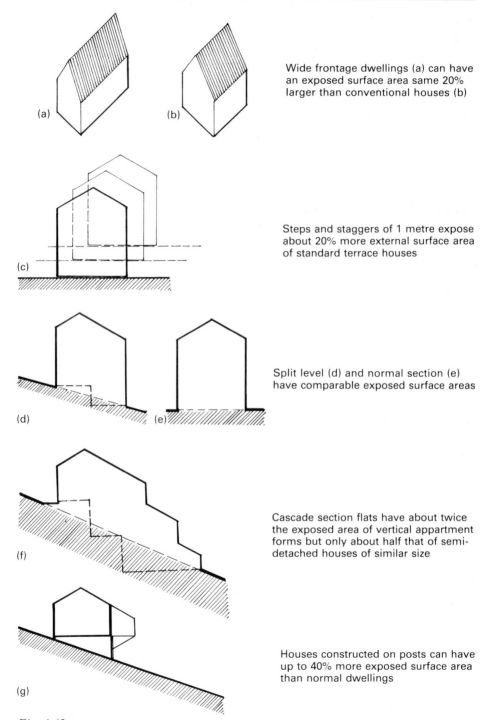

Wide frontage dwellings (a) can have an exposed surface area same 20% larger than conventional houses (b)

Steps and staggers of 1 metre expose about 20% more external surface area of standard terrace houses

Split level (d) and normal section (e) have comparable exposed surface areas

Cascade section flats have about twice the exposed area of vertical appartment forms but only about half that of semi-detached houses of similar size

Houses constructed on posts can have up to 40% more exposed surface area than normal dwellings

Fig. 4.63 Slopes, house types and exposed surface areas

2. The dwelling forms which step and stagger across the contours to keep the ground floor slab close to the natural ground level (such as those at Oakenshaw 6, Redditch) have nearly 19 per cent more exposed surface area for a typical step and stagger of 1 m on each axis.

3. The split level terraces at Cwmbran, with each half floor displaced approximately 1.3 m, have a cross-sectional area 18 per cent larger than comparable flat site terraces. As the asymmetrical roof pitch keeps closer to the usable volume of the dwelling than many other standard roof forms, its total surface area at mid-terrace is 10 per cent less. The end terrace or semi-detached form is comparable to standard dwelling types. Should such a form be used for detached dwellings, the exposed surface area would be about 4 per cent greater than for standard forms.

4. The cascade form in its 'chest of drawers' type section, stepping down the slope in a series of trays as at Central Hill, Lambeth, exposes about twice the amount of its surface skin to the atmosphere as a typical box unit in a vertical block of flats. This profile however is more than twice as efficient as a typical semi-detached house of similar size. If, as at Frankley, Birmingham, the exposed profile is mainly a well insulated roof, then the form is even more efficient.

5. A house constructed on posts will expose not only its walls but an underside equal to the ground floor area of the dwelling. This can add up to 40 per cent on to the area of external envelope exposed to the atmosphere.

As the rate of energy flow is not equal through all parts of a dwelling, it cannot be stated that energy-efficient shapes are directly proportional to their surface area. Similarly, surface area is only one component in the design of a dwelling and energy one component in its running costs. Both however are factors worthy of consideration in the total process of cost-effective house design.

Thermal transmittance and earth shelter

There is one important aspect of design on slopes which influences thermal transmittance: design for earth shelter. There are several factors which greatly affect the extent of earth shelter per unit area including the form of construction, earth composition and water content. Thus the thermal conductivity of water is about twenty-five times that of air, so the wetter the earth the greater its conductivity (within limits). For example, taking the conductivity of dry earth as a factor of 1, 5 per cent moisture raises this to 1.75 and 25 per cent moisture to 2.75 (see Bassett and Pritchard 1968, p 2). Heat transmittance must therefore be calculated separately for each case using texts such as Bassett and Pritchard (1968), Hall (1980) or Pratt (1981).

If a dwelling is burrowed into the earth, more easily achieved on naturally sloping ground than on a flat site, advantage can be taken of the sheltering properties of the soil, especially if the ground is well drained. If the only exposed wall is south-facing with a relatively large proportion of that area glazed, then advantage can also be taken of solar gain. Such construction is rare in Britain where the damp, overcast yet temperate climate does not encourage apparently radical forms of construction, and the traditional masonry building techniques are not well suited to earth sheltered design. One of the few attempts to produce a housing form which acknowledges earth shelter has been the award-winning idea by Terry Farrell and Ralph Lebens in the *Guardian*/Town and Country Planning Association Competition 'Tomorrow's New Community' (*Building Design*, 6 June 1980).

In some other countries earth shelter is standard practice in housing and is common in other buildings, particularly schools, on both flat and sloping sites. An interesting variation on the traditional earth sheltered semi-basement is the Bassano house (1973). This has three kinds of space – a sunspace courtyard which acts as an energy collector and for storage, surrounded by living spaces and underlain by an underground basement which functions as a temperature stabilizer (Los and Pulitzer 1981).

Considerable research on underground building and earth sheltered design is being carried out in the USA, where it is claimed that houses which have been built (invariably one-off private houses) are not appreciably more expensive than equivalent buildings on the flat. In 1981 it was reported that speculative, mass-produced, earth sheltered housing schemes were starting to be built in the USA (*Environmental Comment*, July 1981, p 3).

A survey of existing earth sheltered houses in the southern central United States revealed that even in houses not specifically designed to be energy efficient, the total annual energy usage was decreased by about 40 per cent compared with similar sized houses on open sites. With careful design, this saving can be doubled (see for example the houses in Maryland *Environmental Comment*, July 1981, pp 10–15 and Colorado, Givoni 1980, pp 20–1).

Earth sheltered buildings require less energy both for heating in winter, and where applicable, cooling in summer. This is because the temperature of the surrounding earth is higher in winter and lower in summer than the ambient air temperature to which an ordinary building at ground level is exposed. The difference between inside and outside temperatures, one of the major factors in heat transmittance, is thus reduced.

There may be psychological problems encountered with earth-integrated dwellings, especially because of the lack of immediate contact with the outside. Skilful planning can reduce this. Care is also required to keep ground water out of the building and to reduce condensation within it. A well-drained site is essential for successful earth sheltered design as damp soil will transmit heat much faster than light, dry soil.

The University of Minnesota, through its Underground Space Center, has pioneered research into the viability of earth sheltered design and its work on housing has produced some interesting figures (Minnesota, University of 1979). It should be remembered that the work has been largely based on the north central USA around Minneapolis, where winters are severe (for four months of the year the average temperature is well below 0 °C) and the summers hot and dry (June, July and August each average well above 20 °C with 66 per cent of possible sunshine hours). Such conditions favour earth sheltered structures which respond less dramatically and more slowly to wide temperature variations.

The Center has analysed various models of dwellings from complete underground houses to standard grade level structures. Using the same criteria for each (area, plan form, orientation, energy input) they calculated that a typical North American well-insulated, single-storey dwelling of 140 m^2 built at grade would have an energy deficit during the severe winter months of 6,500 kW hours. During the five summer months such a dwelling would have an energy surplus of over 4,000 kW hours.

A similar sized and orientated structure, but with its north-east and west walls earth sheltered with 500 mm (20 in) of soil placed on an insulated roof, and open south elevation 35 per cent glazed, had a winter energy surplus of over 300 kW hours, and a summer surplus of only just over 700 kW hours. Removing the earth from the roof reduced the winter surplus to 112 kW hours and increased the summer gain to well over 2000 kW hours.

A two-storey earth sheltered structure of similar type to the single storey model was even more energy efficient. With double the floor area, its winter deficit over the smaller house was only some 700 kW hours and its summer surplus 400 kW hours. The increased efficiency was a product of the reduced ratio between exterior surface and floor area.

The example most germane to British usage was that for a typical above grade house with basement (a form not dissimilar to the types developed on sloping sites by firms such as Bovis). In the Minnesota example, a large dwelling of 280 m^2, well insulated, had a winter deficit of 3600 kW hours and a summer surplus of 4700 (i.e. the winter efficiency was almost double that of the above grade bungalow of half the area).

The Center has also classified earth integrated buildings into three architectural types:

1. *Elevational*. All doors and windows are located on one side only (preferably south), while all the other walls and the roof are fully covered by earth.
2. *Atrium*. All the main rooms are placed round an internal courtyard, which may be glazed. The external walls and roof are fully covered.
3. *Penetrational*. Windows and doors are placed around the building in openings which penetrate the earth banks or 'berms'.

The particular choice of type will depend on individual circumstances, but for housing on slopes the elevational type, or a variation upon it, offers immediate advantages, especially if the slope is south-facing. It was this type which was developed by Michael S Milner in the 'Terra Vista' entry for the Housing and Urban Development Passive Solar Design Competition in 1979. With its high-level glazing to the centre of the dwelling and cut-out view from the master bedroom, the design also exhibits certain characteristics of both atrium and penetrational models.

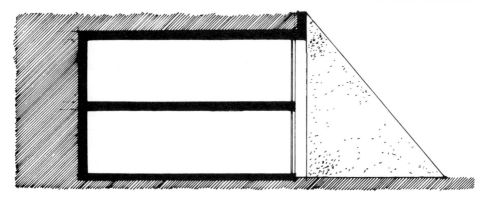

Elevational; particularly suitable on south-facing slopes

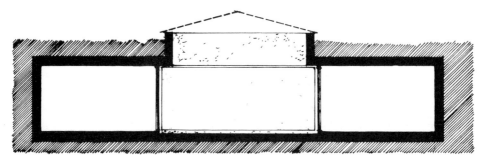

Atrium; courtyard may be open or glazed

Penetrational; easily adapted to sloping sites

Fig. 4.64 Three types of earth-sheltered design as classified by the Underground Space Center, University of Minnesota

The home is located near Frederick in Maryland on a sheltered, well-drained, south-facing slope of nearly 7° (1 in 8.5). Its plan form is typical of many ordinary houses; only the family room has no direct visual contact with outside ground, and even that has natural lighting. The construction is of concrete with 'Bentonite' waterproofer applied on the outside face. Foam insulation and poythene sheeting were then used on the walls before the backfill was firmly compacted. The roofs have an additional layer of polythene between the waterproofer and the insulation, and are covered with 450 mm of soil. Land drains have been used at the bases of all walls and the lower end of each roof.

With triple and quadruple glazed windows and the south-facing greenhouse effect, 75 per cent of the annual heating load is supplied through passive solar gain. A wood-burning stove and heat pump helps with the heating. Cooling is by natural earth contact, the heat pump and is also passively assisted by a 300 mm concrete earth pipe, buried 3 m below grade and sloping away from the house at a distance of 27 m, ending in a vertical air shaft. There is an exhaust fan in the same structure as the chimney to help ventilation. During the cold winter of 1980–1, internal temperatures never dropped below 12 °C and averaged 16 °C. Construction costs were higher than for a similar sized house built above ground, but the developers claim that the idea has been well received and has many advantages in use.

The opportunities for such a solution in Britain are rare. The Terra Vista plan is generous at more than 200 m². The siting and ground conditions are favourable and the climate of the region encourages more thought to be given to the environmental control of the building envelope. As standards of expectation rise and energy becomes more expensive, the design principles of this and similar schemes are to be noted.

Chapter 5

Earthworks on slopes

Introduction

For any housing scheme built on sloping ground, unless the principle of 'houses on stilts' is adopted, such as in the timber framed self-build schemes designed by Walter Segal already described in Ch. 4, there is bound to be some earth manipulation. The degree and effects of such manipulation and methods of dealing with it depend on three factors:
(a) the angles of slope encountered
(b) type of soil
(c) design and density of housing layout.
   In low density schemes at shallow gradients all the earth manipulation can take place as simple landscaping. As gradients and densities increase the amount of earth moving necessary becomes a critical factor of design and cost. The principle of any design should be to produce a solution which does not rely for its success on major earth-retaining structures (especially those exterior to the dwelling) and which requires little transportation of spare material off the site. Any scheme which requires massive earth moving works or large volumes of dumping lacks logical design! Within the scope of this Guide, it should be possible to handle all issues of slope stability and earth retention by one or a combination of the following methods:

1. Natural repose of the manipulated external groundworks.
2. Simple gravity or other retaining walls outside the structure of the dwelling.
3. Simple retention within the conventional form and construction of standard house designs.
4. By retaining walls as part of a specially designed or adapted house type, for example, split level or a full storey buried into the slope.

The third and fourth methods have been covered in Chapter 4. Means of retaining slopes outside the dwelling are described below: the first section considers properties of various soil types, their natural stability, with ways of improving them if necessary. Methods of retaining soil are then explained.

Soils

There are two potential kinds of problem relating to soil stability – erosion and failure. Here we are concerned mainly with the effects and prevention of soil instability. For a discussion of the processes involved see Sparkes (1960) especially Chapter 4, or Young (1972).

Soil erosion

Even on fairly gentle slopes of less than about 5° (1 in 11), earthworks can lead to surface and subsurface instability in the form of erosion or slumping. On a slope under natural conditions erosion due to natural weathering processes takes place at a very slow rate. This may be greatly accelerated by even minor disturbances such as ruts caused by vehicles associated with building or site maintenance, the blocking of a natural drainage channel or even increased pedestrian use. Small channels can become greatly exaggerated by heavy rain causing silting of drains downslope as well as erosion of the slope itself. Light soils are most prone to soil erosion. Where there is little vegetation cover the soil may be removed over the whole slope (sheet erosion) rather than concentration into channels.

There are several factors which can be checked as part of an appraisal to assess the likelihood of soil erosion:

(a) gradients;
(b) type of soil, including evidence of past erosion;
(c) type and extent of vegetation cover;
(d) climate – are heavy downpours characteristic?;
(e) amount of cut-and-fill proposed;
(f) is there any development taking place upslope which could add to erosion problems?;
(g) what land downslope is likely to be affected by erosion from the proposed development site? Are existing water courses adequate to take the extra load? In some countries, developers are liable to prosecution if they cause damage downstream.

The type of soil is a crucial factor in the stability of the ground and its requirements for retention. Indeed, within the design of mass housing on the kind of sloping sites covered by this Guide, the type of soil encountered is probably more important as a factor affecting the stability of ground works than it is with regard to foundation design.

The gradient above which the surface material above bedrock (regolith) is unstable depends on the nature of this material and climate. Non-cohesive soils, mainly sands and gravels, are held together by friction between the particles. They have an angle of repose which is not dependent on the height of the slope, and the greater that angle, the less pressure is exerted on any wall or other structure needed to retain it. Such soils are always stable if the gradient is below the maximum angle of internal friction, regardless of height.

Cohesive soils such as clays are held together by the natural attraction of the particles. This results in the height of the slope affecting the maximum stable angle – the higher the slope, the less steep the gradient at which the soil is stable. Any bank of clay has a tendency to slip and does so in a circular arc or 'slip circle'. In certain clays, normal retaining methods are of little use and piles must be driven down to a level beneath the arc of the slip circle.

The maximum angle of repose of non-cohesive soils can be found by dumping the material in a heap. Some sample tests on soil composition are described in Chapter 2. For cohesive soils, stress tests are conducted in the field or laboratory on undisturbed samples. Problems of measurement increase with mounting clay content and vary according to the type of clay. Stiff clays will permit steep gradients without slippage over small heights. If they are fissured, however, ground water is likely to percolate due to the opening of fissures by relieving lateral stresses with earthworks. Shear strength is therefore reduced.

Hodgkinson (1981e) describes probable angles of repose for various materials:

Wet clay	15°
Very wet clay	18°
Wet sand	25°
Sandy gravel	26–27°
Dry earth or dry clay	30°
Damp sand	33–34°
Dry sand	35–36°
Shingle	40°
Well drained clay or moist earth	45°
Clean gravel in natural deposit	50°

Studies of naturally occurring regoliths, mainly carried out by geologists and geomorphologists, support the general principle that angles of repose are lowest on clay soils and in humid climates and that the presence of stones and to a less extent sand is associated with steeper angles of repose. An angle of 30°–32° is critical for stability in many areas and is common on many resistant rocks (Bunting 1967, Ch. 6; Young 1972).

Slope stability

Subsurface instability and slippage occur where shear stress between layers of the soil is greater than the shear strength. Slippage may not occur if only a very small area is involved as there will be some support from horizontal friction with neighbouring soil zones.

An increase in shear stress can take place in a number of circumstances including the following:

(a) making the slope steeper by earthworks;
(b) building upslope causing additional loading;
(c) changes in drainage patterns caused by earthworks resulting in increased soil weight;
(d) subsidence;
(e) swelling of shrinkable soils.

Once started, slippage may be accelerated by vertical tension cracks filling with water, thus causing a further increase in stress.

A reduction in shear strength can be caused by changes in hydrology such as softening by water uptake, buoyancy and decrease in friction due to a rise in the water table and surface drying and cracking resulting in deep water penetration. Quantitative treatment of these phenomena can be found in books on soil mechanics such as Atkinson (1981).

Shallow landslides are also more likely on areas of drainage concentration. Angle, profile curvature, plan curvature and slope catchment are the most likely causes of moisture concentration (Young 1972; see also Troeh 1964).

Most slopes under natural conditions have a rounded form; convex at the top, maximum plane slope and concave at the foot. This should be imitated by earthworks both for added stability and to harmonize with the natural landscape. The detailed forms of slopes vary greatly (see for example Young 1972, Ch. 12)· but at the scale at which earthworks for housing estates occur it will usually be sufficient to use a simplified form.

Slope stabilization

In certain instances major stabilizing work may be required, although such work is more usually associated with engineering undertakings than with house

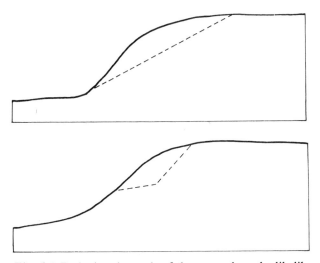

Fig. 5.1 Reducing the angle of slope to reduce the likelihood of slippage

building. Slopes may be strengthened in several ways. The angle may simply be reduced or altered (Fig. 5.1).

An alternative is to load the foot of the slope or provide piling or a retaining wall there.

Removal of water also increases slope stability especially in cohesive soils. There are various types of drain, mostly for use on slopes which are on a larger scale and steeper than is common in most housing estates. One simple type is a buttress drain with trenches at right angles to the contours below the depth of slippage. They are usually stepped along their length. They are commonly 1–2 m wide and about 4–10 m apart. As well as draining the soil, their weight and construction gives physical support to the slope.

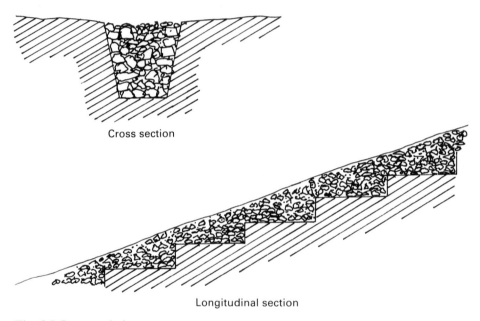

Cross section

Longitudinal section

Fig. 5.2 Buttress drain

Auxiliary drains of rubble-filled trenches may be placed at 45° to the main drains (pointing upslope) to intercept surface run-off. Commonly found dimensions of these are approximately 0.7 m deep, 0.6 m wide and 8 m apart. The crest of a slope is particularly vulnerable for seepage and deep softening followed by slippage, especially if accompanied by softening at the foot of the slope (British Standards Institution 1959).

Surface erosion may be reduced by a number of independent measures.

Terracing. This reduces the speed of water flowing over the slope and can take many forms. Appearance is likely to be important in influencing the design of terracing in housing estates.

Fig. 5.3 Kate's Hill, Dudley, West Midlands. A steep slope of approximately 15 ° is negotiated without drastic, massive retaining structures. Lesser structures of this nature permit more scope for attractive landscaping

Fig. 5.4 Informal terracing with rocks and a strong growth of low bushes prevents erosion and is very attractive here at Aston University, Birmingham

Fig. 5.5 On the other side of the road from Fig. 5.4, concrete surfacing with gaps for bushes is far less attractive

Hard surfacing.   Using bricks, concrete, stone, or other waterproof material, this is a real possibility over small stretches of slope. Care must be taken to prevent water running between the soil surface and the hard surface to avoid undermining. If land form and hydrology are appropriate, waterproof material may be laid just below the brow of the side of the hill opposite to the steep slope to prevent run off from neighbouring land.

Waterproof

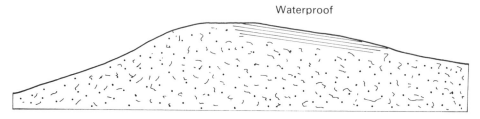

Fig. 5.6 Waterproofing just below the brow of the hill to reduce the chances of slippage on the opposite side

Dams and silt basins.   A simple and effective way of controlling the loss of soil from a site by water erosion is by the construction of low dams, perhaps 2–3 m in height across the exits to water courses. These may be built out of earth with a core of rubble, dumped building materials or even logs. They are easy to construct and can be used as a temporary measure whilst the site is being developed.

156

Turfing. Sometimes only a partial cover is made with intervening spaces being sown with grass seed to save expenditure. Wire netting is occasionally used especially in rocky areas (see the *Journal of the Institute of Landscape Architects*, Nov. 1967). Wattles constructed diagonally down the slope with wire netting between them have been used (*Anthos*, Vol. 4, 1963). Shrubs may be planted diagonally down the slope between the wattles and the wire netting and hollow concrete blocks may be set into the soil with planting of shrubs in the hollows (*Garten und Landschaft*, Feb. 1964)

Mulches. Jute matting is commonly used pegged down with wooden pegs or wire staples to stabilize the soil as grass becomes established. The netting also appears to inhibit the germination of some weeds (Highway Research Board 1959). Straw mulching is still a very common measure to prevent erosion. It also gives protection to germinating grass seeds (Spooner 1969). On steep slopes it is held in position by meshes. It can be used in combination with jute matting. Paper mesh has also been used and so too has glass fibre matting, although it is expensive. Propylene landmesh, a polypropylene netting, may be laid on the vegetation after mowing and is rolled to press it close to the ground, being held in position with hooks. It is claimed that it aids a favourable micro-climate for the establishment of vegetation cover (Hackett *et al*. 1972).

Planting on slopes

Planting has little immediate effect on slope stability and should not be carried out until the angle of repose has been reached (Richardson, *et al*. 1963). Later however the roots have a considerable binding effect and also regulate moisture content.

Hackett *et al*. (1972) recommend plants which propagate vegetatively by stolons for slope coverage and low growing plants rather than trees or shrubs which do not grow so close together. The same authors also give guidance on recommended species and planting methods drawn largely from a study of the banks of the lower reaches of the River Tyne (see also Button 1964).

A particular problem on steep slopes is maintenance such as grass cutting. Low maintenance strains of common grass species have recently been developed in Sweden and (ironically) Holland. The Mommersteg Seed Company now distributes in the UK.

Retention and design

The degree of slope may be such that the ground needs to be retained above the normal angle of repose. Artificial retention will then be necessary.

Retaining walls are of two sorts: gravity retaining walls built of masonry or enclosed soil and relying on mass for their strength and stability and, secondly, cantilever or 'L' shaped retaining walls engineered from reinforced concrete.

Retaining walls of either category can be part of the landscape or can be incorporated within buildings, thus often reducing the need for them in external works. Occasionally slopes will be such that retention is required both within the design of the dwelling and in the external works. It should be stressed however that retaining walls are comparatively expensive and the initial task of the designer should be to avoid their necessity by the plan form of the overall layout and the type of house selected.

A retaining wall must be designed so that it will not overturn or slide; the materials used in construction must not be overstressed, nor must the soil on which it rests. In clay soils, circular slip needs to be avoided. The 'passive' pressure of the earth at the front of the wall must be great enough to resist 'active' pressure at the back. Active water pressure is avoided by the provision of a vertical rubble drainage layer discharging through weep holes (Fig. 5.7). If the retaining wall forms part of a lower storey, lateral drainpipes along the back of the wall lead the moisture into a drain.

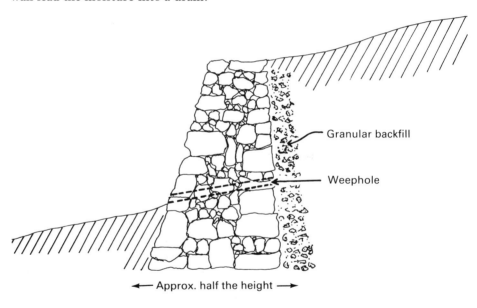

Granular backfill

Weephole

←— Approx. half the height —→

Fig. 5.7 A gravity retaining wall

In normal building work, gravity retaining walls are commonly used for heights of up to 1.8 m and should be adequate for most problems associated with mass housing. Gravity walls are comparatively thick and heavy with the width around half the height and designed so that only compressive stresses are encountered. The design must ensure that the pressure on the earth at the toe is not greater than it can safely resist; also that the resultant thrust on the soil falls inside the middle third of the base and that the wall has no tendency to slide or to slip through shear failure in clay soils. For high walls the rectangular section is not economic as the material at the front adds to the weight and also acts against the resultant force passing within the middle third section.

Crib walls are a form of gravity retaining wall for external works of heights up to 5 m in single width, 9–10 m in double or triple width. They consist of precast

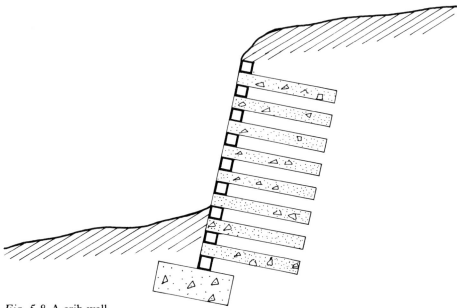

Fig. 5.8 A crib wall

Fig. 5.9 Concrete gravity wall and crib wall on a busy thoroughfare at Erdington, Birmingham. Neither is attractive at present, but the crib wall offers more scope for plant growth

159

reinforced concrete units built up to form open boxes filled with free-draining soil which itself forms part of the retaining wall. Where the height of the wall is less than the depth of the leaders forming the construction, it may be vertical, but usually it is battened to a slope not greater than about 9° (1 in 6) nor less than 7° (1 in 8). The units are built off a concrete strip foundation into which they are keyed.

The accuracy of the calculation of lateral and other pressures will depend on the scale of the works involved. Sometimes they will be very rudimentary for small scale works but for more important retaining structures reference should be made to works on soil mechanics such as Atkinson (1981) or Schofield and Wroth (1968).

In cantilever retaining walls, the resultant of the lateral pressure and weight of wall falls well outside the thickness of the wall. High tensile stresses are thus

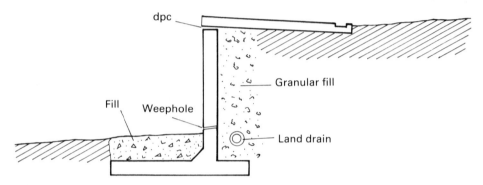

Fig. 5.10 A cantilever retaining wall

Fig. 5.11 Brick-faced reinforced concrete cantilever retaining wall

160

induced and so reinforced concrete is used in an 'L' shaped profile using the vertical retaining arm as a cantilever. Such walls are considerably more economical in their use of space, weight and materials than simple gravity retaining walls but are much more complicated to construct.

In order to avoid the build up of water pressure behind the wall, land drains or weep holes are needed. Land drains should be open jointed leading to a drain and set in coarse inert aggregate. Rodding should be possible. The inside may be painted with pitch epoxy or covered with plastic sheet.

Where lateral pressure is high, a cantilever wall may be stepped. Special bonds of cavity wall such as quetta may be used where the height is up to 3 m. The George Armitage Brick Manufacturing Company has developed brick retaining wall designs with reinforced concrete set into pockets. Reinforced concrete blocks can be a cheaper alternative to bricks, only one leaf being needed. Lifts of masonry should be limited to about 1 m to allow the concrete to be consolidated around the bars to prevent moisture reaching the bars.

Cantilever-reinforced concrete walls are generally up to 3–4 m precast, or reinforced blockwork or 8 m *in situ* walls (Hodgkinson 1981e). Counterfort retaining walls may be used for high lateral pressure.

Costings quoted in Hodgkinson (1981e) show that for low retaining walls of 1 m a mass brick wall or grouted cavity wall is most economical. Pocket walls are cheapest at 2 m and pocket walls with steps at 3–4 m.

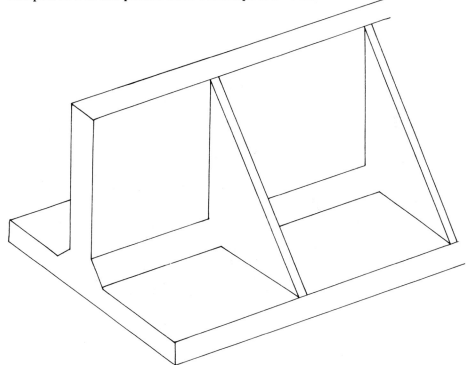

Fig. 5.12 A counterfort retaining wall

Chapter 6

A note on the development industry and market reactions to housing on slopes

Special house designs and the building industry

It has been shown that there is a lot of scope for reducing costs, getting better value for money and making housing on slopes aesthetically more pleasing. There is a great deal of variation in achievement from scheme to scheme when measured against all these criteria. Our findings support a number of criticisms of inefficiency which have been made of the building industry.

Design work is often carried out independent of the financial responsibility usually taken by the builders. This creates obstacles in producing non-standard house types. This, and the conservatism of the building industry, seem to discourage risk taking and innovation, which is reflected in the extreme conservatism of most building societies and perhaps many owners viewing their house in terms of its re-sale potential as well as a place to enjoy. Whether this is due to public satisfaction with present housing or the lack of alternatives to stan-dardised boxes, is open to question. Competition in the private sector is largely comprized of cost for the neighbourhood together with the choice of minor features such as 'Georgian' bow windows or front doors and fitted kitchens. Real competition between house designs in terms of variety and value for money is lacking, even in the private sector.

Even where new designs have been tried such as in several of the examples we have used in this work, these have usually been 'one-off' schemes. It seems to be an extremely inefficient use of design time to use many of these schemes only once.

There is certainly scope for better use of designs skills by the building industry. More co-ordination between architect and builder would go a long way towards this. Perhaps one solution is for builders to employ design skills to offer a range of packages to the buyer. (See for example Bowley 1966, Ch. 16.) This would certainly open up more variety of choice to the house buyer and offer increased efficiency in the use of design skills but would necessitate a radical reorganization of the architectural and other professions.

Much has been written about the economic potential of prefabrication in building – the carrying out of operations separately in time (and usually place) from the final positions of the buildings – and the more far-reaching concept of

162

industrialization involving the organizational principles of industrial production. Developers, both public and private, certainly rely heavily on standardization of components and materials, though some would say not very efficiently. (See for example Bowley 1966, Ch. 12.) Also, it has been argued (Riley 1971) that systems of construction for standard house types with standard exterior finishes could not necessarily compete with more flexible systems of construction.

Therefore, in raising the possibility of new building designs, such as those relating to slope, it is pertinent to ask what would be the effects on the possibilities of standardization and prefabrication. Effects of special house designs on the possibilities of industrialization will follow from the potential for standardization and prefabrication.

In the UK, standardization and prefabrication of components has taken place to a lesser extent than many would have expected. There have been many reasons for this, some of them justifiable. Designers' requirements for flexibility, variety and creativity and the relative cheapness of traditional materials have limited standardization. There is also the paradox that increasing standardization limits the use of components and therefore scale of production. For example, glazed window frames will be less flexible in use than unglazed, due to requirements for different types of glass. Prefabrication too is not desirable beyond certain limits. Increase in size of components makes transport and handling more difficult. Also, the small scale of locally used components may not justify prefabrication, which usually takes place off site in a limited number of places.

The traditional building methods, materials and components still standard practice in Britain would apply in almost the same way to special hill housing as to flat site designs. There are a few clear exceptions – roof trusses in split level dwellings, steps in concrete foundations [for example] – but generally the

Fig. 6.1 Good use is made of roof space and earth shelter . . .

Fig. 6.2 ... adaptation of house type to slope is not incompatible with the use of prefabricated sections. Stockholm

standard components in common use would be applicable to sloping site designs just as for the mass produced flat site house types. This is partly due to the fairly low level of standardization at present practised. Certainly some forms of split level and cascade dwellings would not lend themselves easily to standardization of some larger components. It is possible that other sloping site house types would be developed. For example, the type of split level house with a break in levels at the ridge line may be more adaptable than those split level forms without.

The use of repetitive designs with the resultant savings in labour has probably been a greater incentive for standardization to developers than repetition of components. When breaking away from flat site house types, a developer must produce several different house types for various gradients which considerably multiplies his range of 'standard' types. The cost of design, increased problems of site supervision due to greater range of house types, the possibility of more skilled trades being needed and the costs of promotion are all disincentives. Much 'dimensioning' of building components (fitting them together, usually reducing their size) takes place on site and would be a more skilled job with a greater range of house types.

At least three characteristics of the development firm may be expected to have a bearing on willingness and ability to adapt designs to slope.

1. *Size.* There are certainly more possibilities for standardization in larger firms, but the situation is far more complicated: size is not the sole criterion. Independence of units within a firm also influences the prospects for

innovation. However, marketing facilities and risk of poor sales do favour innovation in larger firms.

2. *Market range*, this is affected by the image of the developer and also by inertia. Perhaps more design staff and more skilled workers are employed by firms at the upper end of the market range.

3. *Public or private sector.* The public sector is to some extent protected from design costs. Some inefficiency may be hidden in the regulations for public sector housing cost control. Public sector reaction to the quite common trade-off between capital and running costs too may be quite different from that of the private sector. There are certainly many examples of capital costs in the public sector having been reduced at the expense of higher running costs. It should be remembered that these rules when applied to housing finance in the private sector – for example by building societies – usually have the same result, although the private sector is less subject to capital cost control except via income of buyers and building society interest rates. Also, considerations of selling price in the private sector often override those of construction cost.

Residents' reactions to housing on slopes

The ultimate test of the viability and desirability of any design must be the users' reactions to it. For housing, this is an extremely complicated question. Attitudes towards housing are likely to be influenced by a larger number of inter-related factors which might include, for example:

(a) the external appearance;
(b) ease and expense of maintenance;
(c) internal layout;
(d) what residents have seen elsewhere before and after buying their house;
(e) changing requirements, for example, more space for a growing family; fewer stairs as people age, new needs for garaging;
(f) view from the house: this may change and so can residents' attitudes towards it;
(g) standard of workmanship on the house and quality of materials.

Attitudes must be a result of a whole series of partly subconscious, changing thoughts reacting on each other in a personal way which are sometimes unclear even to the residents themselves. And it is not only residents who are affected by house design and layout.

From this myriad of only partly specifiable and personal thoughts, house designers finally have the task of trying to sort out which components of house design are likely to get the best reception in both public and private sectors and which designs will be commercially viable. Although a daunting task, it is a necessary one. The results from the kinds of surveys which follow can at best only evaluate satisfaction already achieved rather than probable success with other designs, amongst which are included necessity for adaptation to slope.

Three small personal interview questionnaire surveys covering 112 houses built in the late 1970s were carried out on a public authority housing estate at Frankley and a private sector estate at Harborne (both in the south-western suburbs of Birmingham). The houses at Frankley have already been described in Chapter 4. Those at Harborne consist of two types; one with a bedroom at ground floor level downslope, and two bedrooms, kitchen and car port at first floor level approached from upslope. The second type at Harborne has bedrooms and entrance at ground floor level with a lounge, kitchen and large balcony on the first floor (Fig. 6.3).

Fig. 6.3 One of the house types for which the questionnaire survey was conducted at Harborne, Birmingham

Questionnaire for adapted Harborne housing		*answers* (%)
1. How long have you lived in this house?	less than 6 months	4
	6 months or more	96
2. How does your view of the property now compare with your original impressions?	like it better	54
	dislike it more	4
	no change	42
3. What are its good points?	compact and easy to run	22
	good views	60
	interesting shape	27
	different design	27
	others	62

4.	What are the bad points?	too many stairs	45
		ugly	0
		awkward arrangement of rooms	48
		others	31
5.	Do you think it might be difficult to resell?	yes	34
		no	60
		do not know	6
6.	Would you rather live in a more conventional house?	yes	16
		no	84
		do not know	0
7.	Do you think it sensible to design special house types for difficult sloping sites?	yes	87
		no	0
		do not know	13
8.	Do you think your house is good value for money?	yes	86
		no	7
		do not know	7
9.	What attracted you to buy this house?	unconventional design	20
		special features	7
		best buy available	64
		nothing else in chosen market area	11
		others	44
10.	Would you consider buying another non-conventional house?	yes	66
		no	30
		do not know	4
11.	Can you tell me the composition of your family?	3-person	51
		4-person	42
		5-person	7
	and your position within it?	wife	65
		husband	15
		son/daughter	20
12.	How many bedrooms are there in this house?	3	100

Questionnaire for Frankley housing			*answers* (%)
1.	How long have you lived in this house?	less than 6 months	5
		6 months or more	95
2.	How does your view of the property now compare with your original impressions?	like it better	40
		dislike it more	23
		no change	37

167

3.	What are its good points?	compact and easy to run	3
		good views	41
		interesting shape	20
		different design	37
		others	51
4.	What are the bad points?	too many stairs	54
		ugly	0
		awkward arrangement of rooms	18
		others	28
5.	Would you like to buy this house?	yes	55
		no	38
		do not know	7
6.	Do you think it might be difficult to re-sell?	yes	35
		no	55
		do not know	10
7.	Would you rather like in a more conventional house?	yes	42
		no	54
		do not know	44
8.	Do you think it sensible to design special house types for difficult sloping sites?	yes	80
		no	15
		do not know	5
9.	Do you think your house is good value for money?	yes	42
		no	40
		do not know	18
10.	If before you moved here, you had been looking to buy a house, would you have bought this one or a more conventional one?	this one	33
		more conventional	67
11.	Can you tell me the composition of your family?	2 person	10
		3 person	18
		4 person	22
		5 person	31
		6 person	12
		7 person	7
	and your position within it?	wife	63
		husband	27
		son/daughter	10
12.	How many bedrooms are there in this house?	2	12
		3	73
		4	15

Questionnaire for conventional housing at Harborne		*answers* (%)
1. How long have you lived in this house?	less than 6 months	8
	6 months or more	92
2. What attracted you to buy this house rather than one of the split level designs opposite?	thought the arrangement was better	85
3. What are your opinions on split level designs?	favourable	33
	unfavourable	67
4. Would you consider buying a non-conventional house?	yes	43
	no	57
5. Would you look for one on a sloping site?	yes	31
	no	60
	do not know	9
6. Do you think it sensible to design special house types for difficult sloping sites?	yes	58
	no	30
	do not know	12
7. Can you tell me the size of your family?	1 person	8
	2 person	32
	3 person	34
	4 person	20
	5 person	6
and your position within it?	wife	85
	husband	15
	son/daughter	0

Despite the two adapted estates being of different tenure and quite different house forms there were a number of similarities in the results:

(a) In both cases the opinions of residents tended to become more favourable as time passed (Q. 2)
(b) More attractive features were mentioned than bad ones (Q. 3 and 4), especially good views. It is not clear why the views from Harborne should be more highly valued than Frankley (Figs. 6.4, 6.5 and 6.6). Perhaps residents in the private sector value views more highly.
(c) A substantial number of replies in both cases mentioned too many stairs. At Harborne the only stairs not usual in conventional housing are those outside leading down to the front entrance.
(d) Perceptions of resale potential were remarkably similar despite the very different designs and differences in neighbourhood.

Differences beetween the two surveys may well result from the house designs, neighbourhood and tenure as well as attitudes to house designs on sloping sites:

(a) Generally there was greater satisfaction with the Harborne housing. Was this a result of it being nearer to the conventional or due to them all being owner/occupiers? (Q. 4, 6, 8 and 10 Harborne; Q. 9 and 10 Frankley).

169

Fig. 6.4 General view from the houses surveyed at Harborne, Birmingham. Obviously the views from each house will be different and greatly affected by immediately neighbouring properties. However, this is the general middle and long distance view looking south-east downslope – a quite pleasant open area of the Woodgate Valley to the east, with perhaps a less pleasing assemblage of recent private sector boxes to the west and Selly Oak and Bartley Green in the distance

Fig. 6.5 General view from the houses surveyed at Frankley, Birmingham, looking downslope towards the north: council housing and shopping centre in the foreground, Egg Hill on the horizon

(b) Awkward arrangement of rooms was a more frequent complaint at Harborne than Frankley. The main difference is the reversal of convention, with bedrooms below living rooms at Harborne.

Although in both surveys the great majority of respondents were ladies of the house, there was no statistically significant correlation between any of the ques-

Fig. 6.6 General view from the houses surveyed at Frankley, Birmingham, looking downslope towards the north: council housing and shopping centre in the foreground, Egg Hill on the horizon

Fig. 6.7 Conventional private sector housing on a slope at Harborne, Birmingham

tions on attitudes (Q. 2–10) and the position of the respondent (Q. 11). Also there was no significant correlation between the size of family, the number of children and replies to any of the attitude questions. There was, however, a statistically significant correlation at the 95 per cent level between three- and four-bedroom houses and a favourable answer to question 7 at Frankley. Whether

171

dissatisfaction with design expressed in question 7 was confused with the smaller two-bedroom houses is uncertain.

The third survey of conventional private sector housing adjacent to the special designs at Harborne not surprisingly perhaps showed that reactions to unconventional house design were less favourable than those of residents in the non-standard estate. On the other hand, there was a substantial minority who answered sufficiently favourably to suggest that there is a sales potential both for houses on slopes and for special house designs for slopes. Both Harborne questionnaires taken together indicate that there is some self-selection in that those favouring sloping sites and special house designs are in fact buying them but there is also some potential amongst those living in conventional housing to move to the more unconventional on slopes.

Chapter 7

Conclusions

Design achievement and planning permission

Sloping sites should be regarded as a challenge for the site planner and house designer to realize the full opportunities that they offer – fine views, usually with the opportunity to create visually and socially interesting spaces. The market potential of design effort will not be realized until more attention has been given to the opportunities available with slopes. Most parties in the housing industry – building societies with one or two exceptions, buyers, developers – are conservative. In many towns the most sought-after districts are characterized by their individuality and variety of layouts and houses types, often emphasized by a hill location.

It is a moot point how much longer housing schemes which fail to use site potential should continue to get planning permission. Certainly little true market research has been done either by the development industry or by planning authorities on this point. And the variety and interest of most fashionable residential districts is not reproduced in many newly planned estates and, perhaps even more serious, it is common practice that no attempt is made to do so. Too many developers are content to squeeze as many houses on to the site as is allowed by planning permission. Infill sites often over-exploit an existing good residential environment by fitting in as many houses as possible but new schemes too rarely create an environment equal to those exploited by the infill schemes.

It is the planners' job to regulate these excesses of the market. Too often they allow schemes which only just meet standards of privacy, access, density and other minimum requirements. Would the Department of the Environment back them up if they then started to refuse permission on the grounds that a scheme was simply not the best available for the site? It would place a big responsibility on the planners to decide what was best, but that, presumably, is their job.

It would also mean planners having to be designers rather than just umpires applying rules and standards. For a time at least it would slow down the development industry even more. However, we believe that there are too many examples of planning permission being granted in the interests of short-term expediency, at least partly aided by lack of market investigation. More thought would not only give a better product but in the long run a more economical one too. These arguments apply of course to many developments whether on slopes or not. The problems are, however, exaggerated on sloping land where the results are more prominent visually, particularly left-over corners, awkward junctions and disfigured skylines.

The need to exchange ideas

As well as many thoughtless examples, there are schemes in both public and private sectors which have been carefully and sensitively designed. This book has relied heavily on the example set by some of them. Only a fraction of the many good developments in the UK have been mentioned though the ideas contained in some of those left out are reflected in those included.

Certainly there is a lot to be learned by looking abroad. Designs free of the conservatism and traditions of the UK house building industry and institutions associated with it, in some cases offer a rich source of ideas (even though they may have evolved under another, different set of equally conservative traditions). The use of roof space and attitudes towards partially underground rooms are among the design features which deserve more thought in the UK. Perhaps visions of 'damp cellars' still prevail in the UK. Whether this picture is justified depends on how the design is executed as well as the principle of building below ground level. 'Rooms in the roof' are more commonly an afterthought than part of overall design.

Fig. 7.1 A block of flats grows out of the rock base at Vällingby, Stockholm. Even at high density, much of the rugged natural terrain remains

Fig. 7.2 In the inner suburbs of Stockholm, as here at Kristineberg, flats are the usual dwelling form

The use of space around the building deserves more consideration in the UK. This is often left as useless grassed areas (amenity areas), initially cheap but incurring maintenance costs.

Flats have been more successful in many European countries than in Britain. They have permitted high density, cheap solutions on physically difficult sites and have also allowed the natural terrain to retain some presence. Again, is it the principle that has been wrong for the UK or the way it has been put into practice?

Perhaps all of these faults reflect the priority given to quantity at the expense of quality in British housing during recent decades. Hopefully the pressure for numbers is now reduced.

The costs of building on slopes

Some of the suggestions we have made so far will certainly tend to increase costs. Less use of standard flat site house forms will need greater design effort and closer site supervision. This will, however, be compensated by increasing availability of sloping site designs: more standardization but of rather a different sort. The need for non-standard engineered foundations for some house forms will raise the costs at least until firms acquire experience of them. Most adaptations for slope will result in an increase in the costs of design and for some other adaptations using non-standard parts. As designs become more widely used however, they too will reap the benefits of standardization.

175

Also, the case studies in Chapter 4 have shown that there is scope for reduction in some construction costs on slopes. Within limits set by perceived need or market potential and standards of space, finishes and fittings, the solutions adopted are probably not far above the minimum cost for most of the cases studied. But these limits themselves are important constraints. There have been cases of large wide-fronted houses at right angles to a steep slope – clearly a result of sales potential rather than cost considerations. In fact, the pursuit of minimum cost breaks down on steep and uneven slopes such as at Frankley (Birmingham). St Ann's (Nottingham) and Oakenshaw 5 (Redditch). A high cost has to be incurred to use the site for any kind of housing. Also, particularly at St Ann's, social need and position within the City of Nottingham had an important influence on dwelling type.

Despite these limits on the possibilities of generalizing from the results, each case study showed construction costs to be an important factor. They consistently pointed to certain conclusions.

It makes economic sense to design with the 'grain' of the site, to consider the overall layout and range of suitable house types within the context of the specific location and to marry the scheme to the slope. On relatively gently sloping land of up to about 5° (1 in 11) extra courses of brickwork, usually with a certain amount of cut-and-fill, is the easiest solution in terms of design and execution and is also the cheapest. Particularly where compaction is slow on clays, foundations may have to penetrate through fill down to a load-bearing stratum. The balance between cut-and-fill and extra brickwork depends on ability to compact the soil, tipping facilities for excess fill (which are the main determinant of the cost of cut-and-fill) and, to some extent, professional opinion on the effects of cut-and-fill on the construction standards to be adopted. Although very common, some engineers are sceptical about excessive earth manipulation because of the effects of construction on exposed sub-soils, particularly clays, and the effects on erosion of the building site. Even at a gradient of 5 °, extra construction costs within the site including external works will usually be less than 10 per cent of the construction costs on level ground.

For gradients of approximately 5° (1 in 11) to 9° (1 in 6) there are several possibilities. There will invariably be some earth modelling especially if the slope is near to being at right angles to the house frontages, in order to achieve driveways of acceptable gradients (generally no steeper than about 5° or 1 in 11). Cut-and-fill has been one of the main solutions on such slopes. It does, however, tend to result in some very steep embankments (usually the gardens) which can be a problem aesthetically and for maintenance. On steeper slopes, cut-and-fill can also be expensive. Even under the most favourable conditions on a gradient of 9° (1 in 6), extra costs will be at least 7 per cent of construction costs on level ground (and often up to twice this), excluding external works, services and extra road construction costs. On slopes steeper than about 5°, therefore, the desirability of earth modelling as the prime solution should be questioned on cost as well as several less tangible criteria.

The main alternative on gradients of about 5° to 9° is split level construction.

In fact, it can be used on more gentle slopes though its economic and perhaps aesthetic advantages would be less. Up to 9° there is not a great deal of difference in cost between split level forms and conventional flat site dwellings with cut-and-fill. Superstructure costs tend to be slightly higher for split level forms and substructure costs are considerably higher but these are offset by savings on external works. The advantages of split levels become greater with increasing gradients. Some would argue that they also have maintenance advantages.

On gradients of at least 9° (1 in 6) and up to about 18° (1 in 3), building forms with at least one more storey on the downslope side compared with upslope can be an efficient and aesthetically pleasing solution, or the whole house can be modelled to the slope as at Frankley. Although there is potentially some scope for using the earth as a heat insulator (in a limited way in the UK), there are also problems of damp proofing and the build up of hydrostatic pressure behind the retaining wall. It is quite common to use, perhaps wastefully, the lowest floor for little more than garage space. Extra costs above housing of similar floorspace on level ground may typically be in the range of 11 to 15 per cent.

On the steepest slopes up to 45° a stepped building form is the most common type for mass housing. (See for example Bensemann 1974.) In the UK this kind of design is much more rare than in Scandinavia and Germany for example, though the relative scarcity of such steep sites has no doubt discouraged innovation in the UK. Many other forms of 'one-off' housing forms have been tried (Abbott and Pollit 1980; Wolff 1981). Costs to be expected are at least 25 per cent above housing of similar area on level ground and 40 per cent would not be unreasonable.

Energy implications of adapted designs

There is a tendency to concentrate on capital construction costs at the expense of costs-in-use. Excessive earthworks can have repercussions for erosion and maintenance of retaining walls. Perhaps more significant, and certainly more elusive, are the energy costs dependent on house design. Some designs on slopes, particularly the wide frontage terraced houses, certainly have a greater exposed surface area than is the case for most terraces on level ground. It is not unreasonable to expect their energy consumption to be considerably greater. Steps and staggers may have some effect too. Relatively small differences in energy consumption and maintenance could be quite considerable compared with capital costs of construction. Again, as in relation to other site costs associated with housing, there is the division in responsibility for expenditure between those who commit costs and those who incur them (Simpson 1983 especially Ch. 9).

Capital costs are controlled by the Department of the Environment for the public sector and indirectly by way of prices in the private sector which in turn are dependent on incomes and building society and other interest rates. Costs-in-use are only vaguely known and even more vaguely controlled by a public who do not have the opportunity to inform themselves.

177

However, certain expert experience shows that if ground conditions are right and a more radical approach to design is adopted at the outset, earth shelter need not be more expensive than alternative forms. It does, however, have obvious pitfalls. The reluctance of the British building industry to accept change, the temperate climate and energy prices all cast doubt on the viability of earth shelter as a proposition for mass housing.

Some suggestions for action

1. Many local planning authorities do not demand that private sector developers make good use of site potential in aesthetic and social terms, and almost as many clearly fail to achieve this themselves for their own housing. There is a need for such authorities to review their development control policies to include these factors along with the traditional ones of density, distance between buildings and road standards.

2. To support this view, there is a need for research on the market potential of design effort and achievement. Could extra time spent on design and layout be cost effective? To what extent is the housing available a response to demand? How might demand respond to what could be made available? To investigate these questions would be quite time-consuming and expensive and may involve some risk. The rewards to the private sector for success, however, could be large. As for the public sector, a case could be made for this being part of their duty in order to carry out their development control responsibilities; an attempt to give better public choice and to ensure lasting consumer satisfaction.

3. Even in purely monetary terms, the recent responses to housing on slopes have been inefficient. Hacking away the earth to place on platforms standard flat site houses has in many cases been more costly than adapting house design. Where built form has been adapted, it has nearly always been a 'one-off' design. There is a lot of scope for the pooling of design experiences and standardization and repetition of these 'one-off' designs or certain components of them.

4. The tighter control of capital costs compared with costs-in-use both in the public sector (by Central Government) and the private sector (by the availability of mortgages and rules for their size) has aided designs which are inefficient in terms of their total costs. There is insufficient incentive to reduce costs-in-use, particularly heating by such measures as earth shelter and using dwelling forms which limit the exposed external surface area. Indeed, there is not a great deal of reliable data on the user effects of house design and the potential for energy saving, but what there is indicates the need for further investigation.

Bibliography

Abbott, D. and Pollit, K. (1980) *Hill Housing*, Granada, London.
Architects' Journal (1973) Bristol cliffhanger, **157**, 14 Mar., 604–5.
Architectural Review (1970) St Bernard's Croydon, **CXLVIII**, September, 883.
Atkinson, J. H. (1981) *Foundations and Soils*, McGraw-Hill, Maidenhead.
Atkinson, J. H. and Bransby, P. L. (1978) *The Mechanics of Soils*, McGraw-Hill, London.
Bacon, E. N. (1974) *The Design of Cities*, Thames and Hudson, London.
Bailey, J. (1968) The physical basis of climate, *Architects' Journal*, **148**, 2 Oct., 753–63.
Bassett, C. R. and Pritchard, M. D. W. (1968) *Heating*, Longman, London.
Beddall, J. L. (1950) *Hedges for Farm and Garden*, Faber and Faber, London.
Bensemann, K. (1974) *Planungsgrundlagen für dichte Wohnbebauungen in Hangeladen* (Layout for dense house building on slopes), Institüt für Industrielle Bauproduktion der Universität (TH) Karlsruhe.
Bickerdyke, Allen and Bramble (1974) Brickwork on a sloping site, *Building*, **ccxxvii**, 14 Aug., 71.
Blenk, H. and Trienes, H. (1956) Strömungstechnische Bieträge zum Windschutz (technical properties of wind currents for obtaining shelter), *Grundlagen d. Landtechn.*, 8, I, u, II, VDI-Verl. Düsseldorf.
Bowley, M. (1966) *The British Building Industry*, Cambridge University Press, London.
Brade-Birks, S. G. (1946) *Good Soil*, English Universities Press, London.
British Standards Institution (1945) *Code of Functional Requirements of Buildings: Sunlight: Houses, flats and schools only* (CP 3, formerly CP 5, Ch. 1).
British Standards Institution (1959) *Earthworks*. British Standards Code of Practice, CP 2003, section 3, 25–34; section 4, 34–44; section 8, 65–66.
British Standards Institution (1972) *CP 3: Code of Basic Data for the Design of Buildings*, Ch. V, Part 2, Wind Loads, HMSO, London.
British Standards Institution (1980) *Trees in Relation to Construction*, BS 5837, HMSO London.
Building (1971) Housing down the slope: Cascade housing, Addington near Croydon, **16**, 16 Apr. 90–1.
Building (Second Amendment) Regulations (1981) No 1338, SI, HMSO, London.
Building Research Establishment (1966) Digests 63, 64, 67 (second series) *Soils and Foundations*, Watford.
Building Research Establishment (1983) Digests 274, 275 *Fill*, Watford.
Bunting, B. T. (1967) *The Geography of Soils*, Hutchinson, London.

179

Button, E. F. (1964) Establishing slope vegetation, *Public Works Magazine*, Ridgewood, NJ, USA.

Caborn, J. M. (1965) *Shelterbelts and Windbreaks*, Faber and Faber, London.

Cadman, W. A. (1963) *Shelterbelts for Western Hill Farms*, Forestry Commission Record No 22, HMSO, London.

Campling, J. (1980) Subsidence on clay soils, *Chartered Surveyor*, June, 515–16.

Clarke, G. R. (1957) *The Study of the Soil in the Field*, Oxford University Press, London.

Collmann, W. (1958) *Diagramme zum Strahlungskline Europas* (Diagrams of angles of sunlight in Europe), Ber. D. W. D. Nr. 42.

Contract Journal (1975) Welcomed on the hillside, 27 Nov. 29.

Crawford, D. (ed.) (1975) *A Decade of British Housing 1963–1973*, Architectural Press, London.

Crowe, P. R. (1971) *Concepts in Climatology*, Longman, London.

Davies, A., Wythe, J. and Eley, P. (1978) Cheverton Court, Nottingham, housing for single people, *Architects' Journal*, **167**, 10 May, 901–15.

Davis, Belfield and Everest (1978) Initial cost estimating: the cost of housing, *Architects' Journal*, **167**, 8 Feb., 265–74.

Defant, F. (1949) Zur Theorie der Hangwinde (On the theory of wind on slopes). *Arch. met, Geophys.*, Biok. 1.

Denton, W. A. (1963) The cost plan of Cumbernauld New Town, *Chartered Surveyor*, July.

Department of the Environment (1968) *Final Report of the Working Party on Sewers and Water Mains*, HMSO, London.

Department of the Environment (1971) *Sunlight and Daylight Planning Criteria and the Design of Buildings*, paras 3.5 and 3.6, HMSO, London.

Department of the Environment (1981) *Local Authority Housing Project Control: New Procedures*, Circular 7/81, HMSO, London.

Development Management Working Group (1978) *Value for Money in Local Authority House Building Programmes*, HMSO, London.

Dunbar, M. *et al.* (1973) *A Design Guide for Residential Areas*, Essex County Council, Chelmsford.

Ellis, C. (1980) Do-it-yourself vernacular, *Architects' Journal* **172**, 17 Dec., 1185–1205.

Evans, B. H. (1957) *Airflow around different house shapes*, referred to in **J. F. Griffiths** (1966) *Applied Climatology*, Oxford University Press.

Gammon, J. R. and Thompson, R. (1970) Welsh Village Housing, *Architects' Journal*, **151**, 25 March, 737–52.

Garnett, A. (1939) Diffused light and sunlight in relation to relief and settlement in high latitudes, *Scottish Geographical Magazine*, **55**, 271–84.

Geiger, R. (1965) *The Climate near the Ground*, translated from the 4th German edition of 1961 by Scripta Technica, Cambridge Mass., Harvard University Press.

Gee, K. (1962) Ground slope cost curves, *Chartered Municipal Engineer*, **89**, 299–301.

George, D. J. (1963) Temperature variations in a Welsh Valley, *Weather*, **18**, 270–74.

Gibberd, F. (1962) *Town Design*, (4th edn.) Architectural Press, London.

Givoni, B. (1976) *Man, Climate and Architecture*, Applied Science Publishers, New York.

Givoni, B. (1980) *Earth Integrated Buildings – An Overview*, Applied Science Publishers, New York.

Gloyne, R. W. (1964) Some characteristics of the natural wind and their modification by natural and artificial obstructions. *Scient. Hort*, **17**, 7–19.

Hackett, B., Smith, R. A., Selmes, R. A., Porter, S. and Briscoe, J. (1972) *Landscape Development of Steep Slopes*, Oriel Press, Newcastle.

Hall, F. (1980) *Heating, Ventilating and Air Conditioning*, Construction Press, Harlow.

Halprin, L. (1971) *How to score*, RIBA Journal Annual Discourse, 290–1.

Harrison, A. A., (1967) Variations in night minimum temperatures peculiar to a valley in mid-Kent, *Meteorological Magazine*, **96**, 1142.

Harrison, A. A. (1971) A discussion of the temperature of inland Kent with particular reference to night minima in the lowlands, *Meteorological Magazine*, **100**, 97–111.

Hawkes, D. (1981) Building shape and energy use, in *The Architecture of Energy* (Ed. D. Hawkes and J. Owens,) Construction Press, Harlow.

Highway Research Board (1959) *Asphalt Emulsions*, National Academy of Science, USA, Washington.

Hodgkinson A. (1981a) Notes on Foundations, *Architects' Journal* **173**, 11 March, 457–9.

Hodgkinson, A. (1981b) Building on Clay, *Architects' Journal*, **173**, 11 March, 461–3.

Hodgkinson, A. (1981c) Building on poor ground, *Architects' Journal*, **173**, 18 March, 509–15.

Hodgkinson, A. (1981d) Groundwater, *Architects' Journal*, **173**, 25 March, 557–9.

Hodgkinson, A. (1981e) Building on slopes, *Architects' Journal*, **173**, 8 April, 663–8.

Hodgkinson A. (1981f) Basements, *Architects' Journal*, **173**, 15 April, 707–13.

House Builders, National Association of (1974) *Land Development Manual*, Washington.

Housing, (1979) How to tackle a hillside site, **56**, Nov., New York, 85–91.

Jensen, M. (1954) *Shelter Effect*, Danish Technical Press, Copenhagen.

Jones, M. E. (1976) *Topographic Climates: soils, slope and vegetation* in T. J. Chandler and S. Gregory (Eds) *The Climate of the British Isles*, Longman, London.

Lacy, R. E. (1977) *Climate and Buildings in Britain*, Building Research Establishment (Department of the Environment), London.

Lawson, T. (1968) Air Movement and Natural Ventilation: Wind Tunnel List, A. J. Handbook Building Environment, section 3, *Architects' Journal*, 5 Oct.

Los, S. and Pulitzer, N. (1981) *An Italian experience of bioclimatic design*, in D. Hawkes and J. Owens *The Architecture of Energy*, Construction Press 1981, Harlow.

Lynch, K. (1971) *Site Planning*, MIT Press, Cambridge, Massachusetts.

Lynes, J. (1968) Sunlight direct and diffused, A. J. Handbook Building Environment, section 2, *Architects' Journal* 5 Oct.

Madge, J. (1975) Housing at Langdon Hills, Basildon, *Architects' Journal*, **162**, 2 July, 19–35.

Menzies, J. B. (1971) Wind damage to buildings, *Building*, 27 Aug.

Ministry of Agriculture, Fisheries and Food (1968) *Fixed equipment of the farm, leaflet 15, Shelterbelts for farmland*, HMSO, London.

Minnesota, University of, (1979) *Earth Sheltered House Design*, Underground Space Center.

Morris, R. E. and Barry, R. G. (1963) Soil and air temperatures in a New Forest Valley, *Weather*, **18**, 325–30.

Muncey, R. W.R. (1979) *Heat transfer calculations for buildings*, Applied Science Publishers.

National Building Agency (1976) Trends in Housing and Construction, London.

National Building Council (1974) *Registered House Builders Handbook*, London.

Neylan, M. (1966) Housing at Harlow: Bishopsfield and Charters Cross, *Architectural Review*, July, 39–41.

181

Olgyay, V. (1963) *Design with Climate*, Princeton University Press, Cambridge Massachusetts.

Oslo Kommune (1980) Holmlia – en ny norsk by.

Pedgley, D. E. (1974) Field studies of mountain weather in Snowdonia, *Weather*, **29**, 284–97.

Phippen, Randall and Parkes (1982) Housing at Broadfield 5, Crawley, *Housing Review*, July/August, 127–9.

Plumb, C. (1976) Queensmere Housing Estate, Wimbledon, *Architects' Journal*, **164**, 17 Nov., 931–45.

Post, E. R., McCoy, P. T., Ruby, R. J. and Coolidge, D. O. (1978) *Cost Effectiveness of Driveway Slope Improvements*, Transport Research Record, Washington DC, 14–19.

Pratt, A. W. (1981) *Heat Transmission in Buildings*, John Wiley, Chichester.

Reynolds, E. C. (1979) A report on tree roots and building development, Report for the Department of the Environment, HMSO, London.

Rock, D. (1973) Braving the slopes, *Built Environment*, 2, 135.

Richardson, E. G. Diseker, E. G. and Henderson, B. H. (1963) Crown vetch for highway bank stabilisation in the Piedmont Uplands of Georgia, *Agronomy Journal*.

RICS Design/Cost Research Working Party (1965) Cost Research Paper: basement construction, *Chartered Surveyor*, March.

Riley, J. (1971) All round flexibility in systems building, *Building Technology and Management*, April, **9**, 8.

Schofield, A. N. and Wroth, C. P. (1968) *Critical State Soil Mechanics*, McGraw-Hill, London.

Schütte, K. (1943) Die Berechnung der Sonnenhöhen für beliebig Geneigte (calculation of sunlight angles for any incline) *Eben, Ann. d. Hydr.*, **71**, 325–8.

Scott and Furphy Engineers (1979) *Design and Siting Guidelines: Highly Dissected Hill Country partly or wholly cleared*, Town and Country Planning Board, Melbourne.

Scottish Development Department (1972) *North Slope Study*, HMSO, Edinburgh.

Scottish Development Department (1973) *Threshold Analysis Manual*, HMSO, Edinburgh.

Scottish Development Department (1975) *New House Building – cost control procedures and indicative costs*, Circular 55/1975, HMSO, Edinburgh.

Seeley, I. H. (1976) *Building Economics* (2nd edn,) Macmillan, London.

Simounet, R. (1982) Gradins, avec ou sans pente (Tiers, with or without slope), *Technique et Architecture*, **341**, April/May, 93.

Simpson, B. J. and Purdy, M. T. (1982) A right angle on cost and design, *Surveyor*, 12 Feb. 8–10.

Simpson, B. J. (1982) Sweden takes steps to build on slopes, *Surveyor 11 Nov.*, *12–13*.

Simpson, B. J. (1983) *Site Costs in Housing Development*, Construction Press, Harlow.

Sparkes, B. W. (1960) *Geomorphology*, Longman, London.

Spooner, P. (1969) *Highway landscape design*. Australian Road Research Board, Canberra.

Stone, P. A. (1980) *Building design evaluation: costs-in-use* (3rd edn) Spon, London and New York.

Svenska Byggnadsentreprenoerfoeriningen (1976) Produktionsanpassad utformning av vaegars oever -och underbyggnader (The design of roads with a view to production considerations), Stockholm.

Timms, W. and Son (Builders) Ltd. (1981) *Arden Estate, Highlands, Banbury*, report by the Charter Design Group for Cherwell District Council, Banbury.

Trickey, G. G. (1975) Housing Cost Yardstick Technical Study 2. The design of economic dwelling forms, *Architects' Journal*, **162**, 193–5.

Troeh, F. R. (1964) Landform parameters connected to soil drainage, *Proc. Soil Sci. Soc. Am.*, **28**, 808–12.

Wolff, R. (1981) *Häuser am Hang* (Houses on Slopes), Callwey, München.

Young, A. (1972) *Slopes*, Longman, London.

Index

References in italics to diagrams or photographs